NORTH AMERICAN SNJ / T-6 TEXAN
PILOT'S FLIGHT OPERATING INSTRUCTIONS

by United States Army Air Forces
and
United States Navy

AN 01-60FE-1

PILOT'S FLIGHT OPERATING INSTRUCTIONS

FOR

ARMY MODEL
AT-6C

NAVY MODEL
SNJ-4

BRITISH MODEL
HARVARD IIA

AIRPLANES

Commanding Officers will be responsible for bringing this Technical Order to the attention of all pilots cleared for operation of the subject aircraft as well as those undergoing Transition Flying Training as contemplated in AAF Regulation 50-16.

Appendix I of this publication shall not be carried in aircraft on combat missions or when there is a reasonable chance of its falling into the hands of the enemy.

Published under joint authority of the Commanding General, Army Air Forces, the Chief of the Bureau of Aeronautics, and the Air Council of the United Kingdom.

NOTICE: This document contains information affecting the national defense of the United States within the meaning of the Espionage Act, 50 U. S. C., 31 and 32, as amended. Its transmission or the revelation of its contents in any manner to an unauthorized person is prohibited by law.

FORT WAYNE PRINTING COMPANY, INC.
FORT WAYNE, INDIANA 1-10-47 2000

5 JANUARY 1945
REVISED 30 AUGUST 1945

POLICY GOVERNING DISTRIBUTION AND USE OF THIS PUBLICATION

Instructions Applicable to U. S. Army Personnel:

1. This publication is intended for technical aid and education of military and civilian personnel engaged in promoting the war effort. Its maximum distribution and use is therefore encouraged. However, since the publication is "restricted" within the meaning of AR380-5, the following security regulations will be observed:

a. *Members of Armed Forces and civilian employees of War Department* will be given access to this publication whenever required to assist in the performance of their official duties (including expansion of their knowledge of AAF equipment, procedures, etc.).

b. *Personnel of War Department contractors and subcontractors* may be given possession of this publication, on a loan basis, or knowledge of its contents, only when required to assist in the performance of War Department contracts. Releases will be made in accordance with the requirements of T. O. No. 00-5-2.

c. *Representatives of other governments* will be given possession of this publication, or knowledge of its contents, only in accordance with AAF Letter No. 45-6.

2. This publication is restricted because the information contained in it is restricted. It does not follow that the physical article to which it relates is also restricted. Classification of the materiel or component must be ascertained independently of the classification of this document.

3. Neither this publication nor information contained herein will be communicated to press or public except through Public Relations channels.

Instructions Applicable to U. S. Navy Personnel:

1. Navy Regulations, Article 76, contains the following statements relating to the handling of restricted matter:

"Par. (9) *(a)*. Restricted matter may be disclosed to persons of the Military or Naval Establishments in accordance with special instructions issued by the originator or other competent authority, or in the absence of special instructions, as determined by the local administrative head charged with custody of the subject matter."

"*(b)* Restricted matter may be disclosed to persons of discretion in the Government service when it appears to be in the public interest."

"*(c)* Restricted matter may be disclosed, under special circumstances, to persons not in the Government service when it appears to be in the public interest."

2. The Bureau of Aeronautics Aviation Circular Letter No. 90-44 contains the following paragraph relative to the use of aeronautical technical publications:

"Par. 8. *Distribution to All Interested Personnel.* In connection with the distribution of aeronautical publications within any activity, it should be borne in mind by the offices responsible for such distribution that technical publications, whether confidential or restricted, are issued for use not only by officer personnel, but also by responsible civilian and enlisted personnel working with or servicing equipment to which the information applies."

3. Disclosure of technical information in this publication may not be made to representatives of foreign governments except in instances where those foreign governments have been cleared to receive information concerning all equipments covered by this publication.

Instructions Applicable to British Personnel:

FOR OFFICIAL USE ONLY.—Not to be communicated to anyone outside of His Majesty's Service. Not to be published. The information given in this document is not to be communicated, either directly or indirectly, to the press or to any person not holding an official position in His Majesty's Service.

LIST OF REVISED PAGES ISSUED

NOTE: A heavy black vertical line to the left or in outer margin of text on revised pages, indicates extent of revision. This line is omitted where more than 50 percent of page is revised. A black horizontal line to the left of page numbers listed below indicates pages revised, added or deleted by current revision. This line is used only on second and subsequent revisions.

AAF

ADDITIONAL COPIES OF THIS PUBLICATION MAY BE OBTAINED AS FOLLOWS:

AAF ACTIVITIES.—In accordance with T. O. No. 00-5-2, Air Inspectors will submit requisitions (AAF Form 104B) to:

Commanding General
Fairfield Air Technical Service Command
Patterson Field, Ohio
Attn: Publications Distribution Branch

NAVY ACTIVITIES.—Submit requests to Chief, BuAer, Navy Department, Washington, D. C., Attention: Publications Branch on order form NAVAER-140. For complete listing of available material and details of distribution see Naval Aeronautic Publications Index, NavAer 00-500.

BRITISH ACTIVITIES.—Submit requirements on Form 294A, in duplicate, to the Air Publications and Forms Store, New College, Leadhall Lane, Harrogate, Yorkshire, England.

TABLE OF CONTENTS

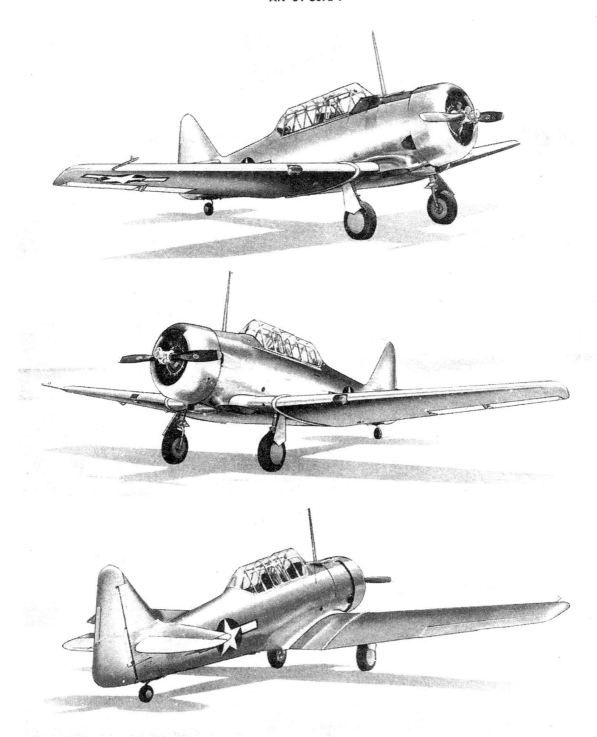

Three Views of AT-6C

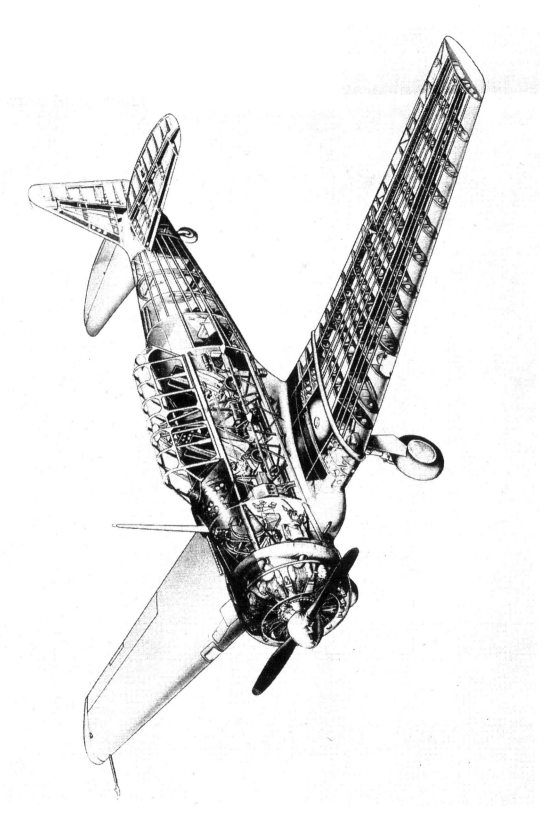

Phantom View of AT-6D

Three Views of AT-6D

SECTION I
DESCRIPTION

1. GENERAL.

AT-6C and SNJ-4 (Navy) airplanes are two-place, dual controlled, single-engine, low-wing monoplanes designed as advanced trainers with provisions for the installation of bomb carrying and gunnery equipment. The front fuselage section houses the front and rear cockpits and all the controls and equipment for operating the airplane. The baggage compartment and lift and mooring tube are contained in the rear fuselage section. The airplane has a wing span of 42 feet, 1/4 inch; a length of 28 feet, 11-7/8 inches; a height (tail up) of 12 feet, 9-1/4 inches; and weighs (normal gross) 5300 pounds.

2. DESCRIPTION OF CHANGES.

A major production change in movement of control surfaces to improve the spin characteristics of the airplane divides them into two basic groups as listed below.

The airplane can be identified by movement of the aileron tabs. Booster tabs on Group I airplanes will move in opposite relation to the aileron while trim tabs on Group II airplanes are fixed. For effectiveness of these changes, refer to section II, paragraph 13.

	Group I Airplanes	Group II Airplanes
Rudder travel (from airplane center line)	35 degrees	30 degrees
Aileron Travel		
Up	30 degrees	15 degrees
Down	15 degrees	15 degrees
Aileron tabs	Booster	Trim
Tail wheel travel (from airplane center line)	30 degrees	*15 degrees

*Tail wheel—rudder travel ratio, 2:1.

Note

On Group II airplanes the rudder pedal neutral position is moved aft one inch to provide full rudder throw by pilots of very short stature.

3. FLIGHT CONTROLS.

The ailerons, elevators, and rudder are conventionally operated from either cockpit by a control stick and rudder pedals. A flap control handle is mounted on the control shelf at the left side of each cockpit. A surface control locking mechanism is left and forward of the front cockpit control stick base. The controls are locked in this manner: neutralize the rudder pedals, push the control stick forward of center, pull up and aft on the lock handle, engage the control stick in the lock recess, and engage the lock plunger. To release, push the lock control handle forward and down. Aileron trim or booster tab adjustments are made at the tab only; rudder and elevator trim tabs are adjusted by control wheels on the left side of each cockpit. Elevator trim wheel is marked "NEUTRAL", "TH", and "NH"; rudder trim wheel is marked "NEUTRAL", "L", and "R". The rear cockpit control stick, when not in use, is stowed in a socket at the left side of the cockpit.

4. LANDING GEAR.

a. CONTROL. (See figures 5 and 8.)—A control lever for the hydraulically operated main landing gear is mounted on the control shelf at the left side of each cockpit. The front cockpit control has three positions, "UP", "DOWN", and "EMERGENCY" (used to manually lock the gear in the down position). This control will extend or retract the gear. Controls must remain in their "UP" or "DOWN" positions when the gear is operated as there is no neutral position. The control in the rear cockpit will only extend the gear. The non-retractable tail wheel is steered by the rudder pedals within a 15 degree arc (30 degrees on Group I airplanes) in either direction and becomes free-swiveling beyond that point.

b. POSITION INDICATOR. (See figure 5.) Mechanical position indicators on the forward end of the control shelf in the front cockpit indicate the travel and position of the main landing gear at all times.

c. WARNING HORN.—A warning horn is mounted in the overturn structure above the rear instrument panel. If the landing gear is not locked in the down position when the throttle is retarded for landing, the horn will vibrate.

CAUTION

Do not operate the landing gear control when airplane is on the ground, as there is no safety provision to prevent the gear from retracting.

5. BRAKES.

(See figure 1.)

A separate hydraulic system is employed for operating the brakes which are of the reversible, Hayes internal expanding type. Brake pedals are incorporated in the rudder pedal assemblies of both cockpits. A handle for setting the parking brakes is located just below the electrical control panel in the front cockpit only; however they may be released from either cockpit by depressing the pedals. The parking brakes are set by depressing the brake pedals, pulling out the handle, releasing the pedals, and then releasing the handle.

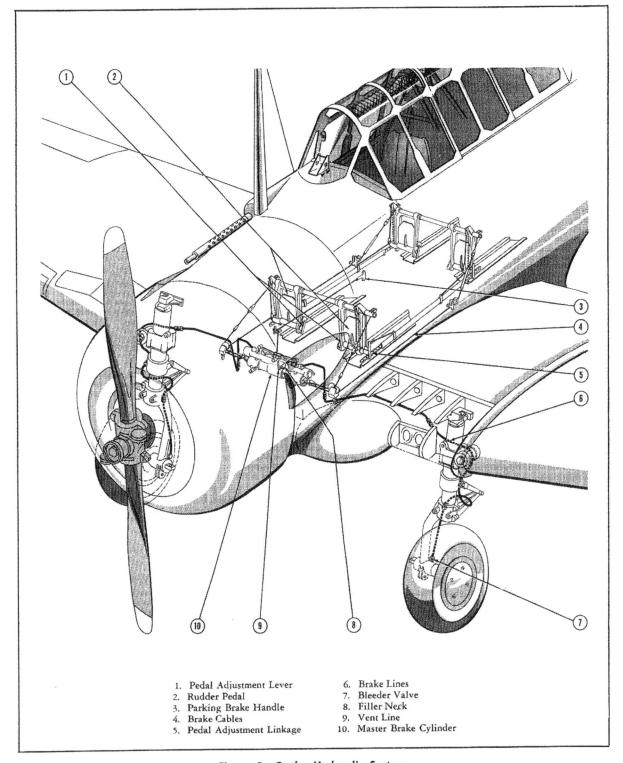

1. Pedal Adjustment Lever
2. Rudder Pedal
3. Parking Brake Handle
4. Brake Cables
5. Pedal Adjustment Linkage
6. Brake Lines
7. Bleeder Valve
8. Filler Neck
9. Vent Line
10. Master Brake Cylinder

Figure 1 — Brake Hydraulic System

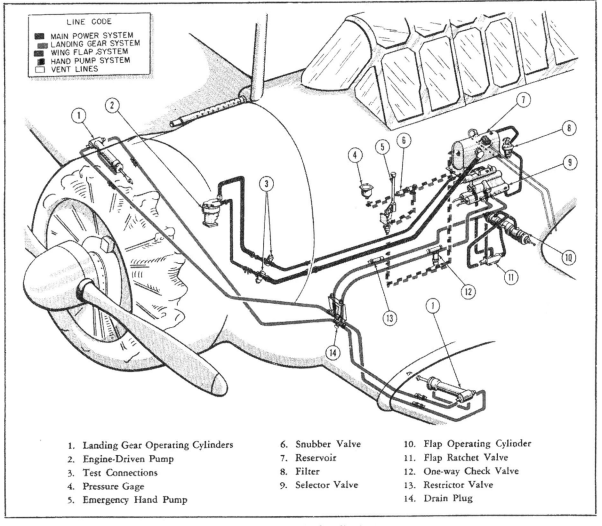

1. Landing Gear Operating Cylinders	6. Snubber Valve	10. Flap Operating Cylinder
2. Engine-Driven Pump	7. Reservoir	11. Flap Ratchet Valve
3. Test Connections	8. Filter	12. One-way Check Valve
4. Pressure Gage	9. Selector Valve	13. Restrictor Valve
5. Emergency Hand Pump		14. Drain Plug

Figure 2 — Main Hydraulic System

6. MAIN HYDRAULIC SYSTEM.

(See figure 2.)

The main hydraulic system is provided to operate the main landing gear and wing flaps. Pressure is controlled by a power control lever on the control shelf of each cockpit; when pressed, hydraulic power is available for approximately two minutes before the control automatically disengages. Operation of the flaps and landing gear is controlled by individual levers on the control shelf of each cockpit. The flap control has three positions, "UP", "LOCKED", and "DOWN". The "LOCKED" position is used to lock the flaps in any intermediate position. It is necessary to leave the control in the "UP" or "DOWN" position when full retraction or extension is desired as there is no neutral position. An emergency hand pump, located just left of the pilot's seat in the front cockpit, is provided for emergency operation of the flaps and landing gear. A pressure gage on the forward end of the front cockpit control shelf indicates the pressure in the main hydraulic system when the power control lever is engaged.

7. POWER PLANT.

a. ENGINE.—The airplane is powered by a Pratt and Whitney R-1340-AN-1, nine-cylinder, air-cooled, radial engine equipped with a Hamilton Standard constant-speed propeller and an up-draft type carburetor containing an idle cut-off. A quadrant on the left side of each cockpit contains the throttle, mixture, and propeller control levers. Creepage of the controls is prevented by a disc-type friction clutch at the bottom of the front cockpit quadrant only.

b. FUEL AND OIL.
  Fuel: Specification No. AN-F-25, grade 87
  Oil: Specification No. AN-VV-O-446a, grade 1120
     (S) and AN-O-5, 1100 P (W)

c. THROTTLE CONTROL.—The throttle controls on the two quadrants are linked by rods; the forward position is "OPEN", the aft position "CLOSED". A toggle-type stop on the front quadrant restricts movement of the controls so that 36 in. Hg is not exceeded at sea level take-off. The stop may be released only on the front quadrant for further throttle advancement in case of emergency.

d. MIXTURE CONTROL.—The two mixture controls are linked by rods and the positions are: forward, "RICH"; aft, "LEAN". Movement of the controls to the "LEAN" position is restricted by a spring-loaded ratchet mounted on the forward face of the front control. This ratchet can be released only at the front quadrant, thus the mixture may be enriched or leaned with the front control but enriched only with the rear control. The idle cut-off becomes effective when the controls are at the extreme "LEAN" position.

e. PROPELLER CONTROL. — The positions of the propeller controls are: forward, "INCREASE RPM"; aft, "DECREASE RPM". Movement of the controls operates valves in the propeller governor which controls the blade angle of the propeller. Blade angles of the propeller are from 11-½ degrees in the low pitch position to 27 degrees in high pitch.

f. CARBURETOR AIR CONTROL. *(See figure 5.)*—The carburetor air temperature control quadrant is lo-

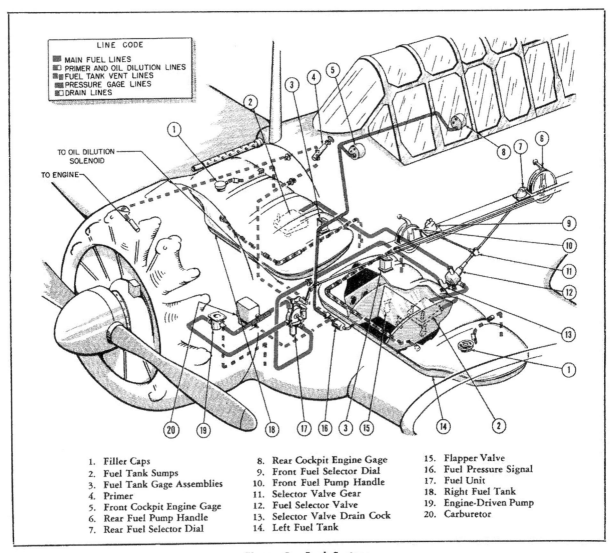

LINE CODE
■ MAIN FUEL LINES
▨ PRIMER AND OIL DILUTION LINES
▥ FUEL TANK VENT LINES
▦ PRESSURE GAGE LINES
▨ DRAIN LINES

TO OIL DILUTION
SOLENOID

TO ENGINE

1. Filler Caps	8. Rear Cockpit Engine Gage	15. Flapper Valve
2. Fuel Tank Sumps	9. Front Fuel Selector Dial	16. Fuel Pressure Signal
3. Fuel Tank Gage Assemblies	10. Front Fuel Pump Handle	17. Fuel Unit
4. Primer	11. Selector Valve Gear	18. Right Fuel Tank
5. Front Cockpit Engine Gage	12. Fuel Selector Valve	19. Engine-Driven Pump
6. Rear Fuel Pump Handle	13. Selector Valve Drain Cock	20. Carburetor
7. Rear Fuel Selector Dial	14. Left Fuel Tank	

Figure 3 — Fuel System

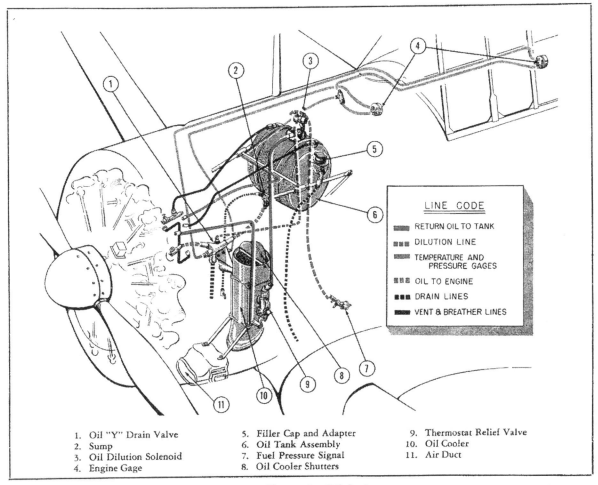

1. Oil "Y" Drain Valve
2. Sump
3. Oil Dilution Solenoid
4. Engine Gage
5. Filler Cap and Adapter
6. Oil Tank Assembly
7. Fuel Pressure Signal
8. Oil Cooler Shutters
9. Thermostat Relief Valve
10. Oil Cooler
11. Air Duct

Figure 4 — Oil System

cated at the left side of the front cockpit. When the control is in the "COLD" position, the gate in the carburetor air duct is open to permit cold air entrance; when it is in the "HOT" position, the gate is closed and hot air enters from the exhaust manifold shroud.

g. STARTER CONTROL. (See figure 13.)—A foot pedal for electrical control of the starter is mounted between the rudder pedals in the front cockpit. Pressure on the heel of the pedal energizes the starter and pressure on the toe of the pedal engages the starter with the engine.

b. MANIFOLD PRESSURE GAGE DRAIN. (See figure 5.)—A manifold pressure gage drain is located on the left side of the front cockpit. This drain should be operated for 5 seconds at engine warm-up in order to expel moisture from the line.

i. ENGINE PRIMER. (See figure 7.)—The manually operated primer pump is installed directly below the front cockpit instrument panel. Pushed in and turned to the right, the handle is in the "OFF", locked position.

To unlock, push the handle in and turn to the left.

8. FUEL SYSTEM.
(See figure 3.)

a. GENERAL—Two 55 US (46 Imperial) gallon fuel tanks are housed in the wing center section structure. A 20 US (16.7 Imperial) gallon reserve compartment is contained in the left tank. Controls for the system are comprised of a hand fuel pump handle and a fuel selector control at the left of each cockpit and an engine primer in the front cockpit. Fuel contents gages and a fuel switch-over signal lamp comprise the system instruments. Fuel is inducted into the carburetor by the engine-driven fuel pump from either tank through the fuel selector valve and the fuel unit. In the event of failure of the engine-driven fuel pump, fuel is supplied to the carburetor by the fuel unit, pressure being applied by the hand pump.

b. FUEL SWITCH-OVER SIGNAL. (See figure 7.)—A signal lamp on the right side of the front cockpit instrument panel will light when the carburetor fuel

Figure 5 — Left Side Front Cockpit

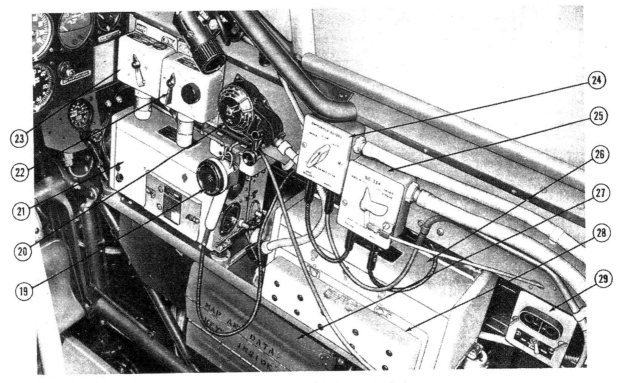

Figure 6 — Right Side Front Cockpit

POWER PLANT CONTROLS

1. Hydraulic Power Control
2. Flap Control
3. Flight Report Case
4. Landing Gear Control
5. Hydraulic Hand Pump
6. Fuel Selector
7. Carburetor Air Temp Control
8. Elevator Trim Tab Control
9. Rudder Trim Tab Control
10. Engine Control Quadrant
11. Blind Flying Hood Release
12. Manifold Pressure Gage Drain Valve
13. Flap Position Indicator
14. Bomb Control Quadrant
15. Landing Gear Position Indicator
16. Hand Fuel Pump Handle
17. Hydraulic Pressure Gage
18. Gun Sight
19. Microphone
20. Receiver Tuning Dial

21. Radio Transmitter
22. Radio Receiver Switch
23. Transmitter Modulator Switch
24. Radio Filter Box
25. Radio-Interphone Selector Switch
26. Radio Receiver
27. Map and Data Case
28. Receiver Coil Unit
29. British Interphone Switch
30. Electrical Control Panel
31. Fuel-Air Ratio Gage
32. Altimeter Correction Chart
33. Ignition Switch
34. Bank and Turn Indicator
35. Clock
36. Altimeter
37. Air-Speed Indicator
38. Suction Gage
39. Magnetic Compass
40. Directional Gyro
41. Camera Signal Light

42. Gyro Horizon
43. Radio Call Plate
44. Rate of Climb Indicator
45. Tachometer
46. Cylinder Head Temp Gage
47. Carburetor Mixture Temp Gage
48. Oil Temp, Fuel and Oil Pressure Gage
49. Manifold Pressure Gage
50. Fuel Switch-over Signal Light
51. Compass Correction Chart
52. Oxygen Pressure and Flow Gage
53. Bomb Release Switch
54. Oxygen Regulator Control
55. Gun Trigger Switch
56. Recognition Light Switches
57. Engine Primer
58. Accelerometer
59. Gun Charger
60. Oil Cooler Shutter Control
61. Parking Brake Handle

Figure 7 — Center Front Cockpit

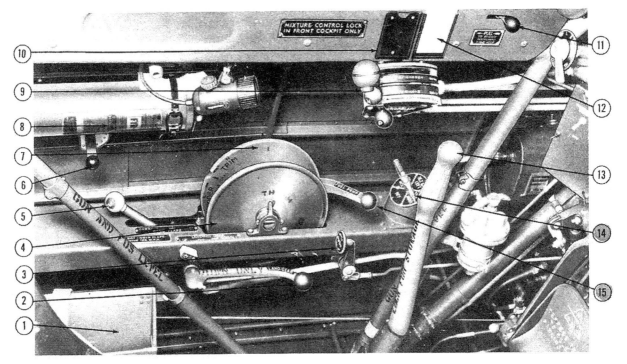

Figure 8 — Left Side Rear Cockpit

Figure 9 — Right Side Rear Cockpit

POWER PLANT CONTROLS

1. Flight Report Case
2. Landing Gear Controls
3. Hydraulic Power Control
4. Elevator Trim Tab Control
5. Flap Control
6. Ventilator Door Handle
7. Rudder Trim Tab Control
8. Fire Extinguisher
9. Engine Control Quadrant
10. Altimeter Correction Chart
11. Blind Flying Hood Release
12. Compass Correction Chart
13. Control Stick (Stowed)

14. Fuel Selector Valve
15. Hand Fuel Pump Handle
16. Bank and Turn Indicator
17. Ignition Switch
18. Air-Speed Indicator
19. Altimeter
20. Radio Call Plate
21. Clock
22. Spare Lamp
23. Directional Gyro
24. Magnetic Compass
25. Gyro Horizon
26. Suction Gage

27. Rate of Climb Indicator
28. Tachometer
29. Oil Temp, Fuel and Oil Pressure Gage
30. Electrical Control Panel
31. Oxygen Pressure and Flow Gage
32. Oxygen Regulator Control
33. Interphone Amplifier Switch
34. Microphone
35. Receiver Tuning Switch
36. Receiver Tuning Dial
37. Radio-Interphone Selector Switch
38. Volume Control

Figure 10 — Center Rear Cockpit

Figure 11 — Front Cockpit Electrical Control Panel and Recognition Light
Switch Box

pressure falls below 3 lb/sq in. When the fuel supply is exhausted, the fuel pressure will drop and cause the lamp to light approximately 10 seconds before engine failure. A testing switch for the lamp is located on the front cockpit electrical control panel.

c. HAND FUEL PUMP. (See figures 5 and 8.)—The hand fuel pump is operated to obtain fuel pressure when starting the engine, or in case of engine-driven fuel pump failure. An operating handle is located on the control shelf of each cockpit. Insufficient operation of the hand fuel pump will be indicated by the fuel pressure signal lamp.

d. FUEL SELECTOR VALVE. (See figures 5 and 8.) —Selection of fuel supply is controlled by a selector valve control located on the control shelf of each cockpit. Fuel flow markings are: "RESERVE", "LEFT", and "RIGHT". An "OFF" position is provided to completely shut off the flow of fuel.

e. FUEL CONTENTS GAGES. (See figure 19.)—Two float-type fuel contents gages are located one on either side of the front cockpit seat and are visible from the rear cockpit with approximately 5 gallons parallax error.

9. OIL SYSTEM.
(See figure 4.)

a. GENERAL.—A 10 US (8-1/2 Imperial) gallon oil tank provides the reserve supply for the engine lubricating system. Pressure and temperature indicators are contained in the engine gage units on the two instrument panels. The oil cooler shutter control in the front cockpit is the only manually operated oil system control and

is provided for operation in extreme cold weather only. When the handle is in the up position, the shutters are "CLOSED" and when in the down position, the shutters are "OPEN". The control quadrant is notched to permit setting in any intermediate position.

b. OIL DILUTION SYSTEM.—The oil dilution system is controlled by a switch on the front cockpit electrical control panel. With this switch in the "ON"

Figure 12 — Rear Cockpit Electrical Control Panel

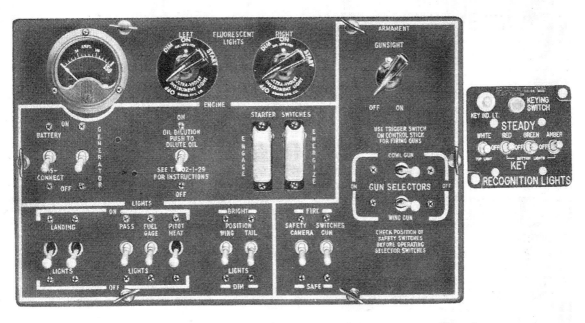

Figure 11a — Front Cockpit Electrical Control Panel and Recognition Light
Switch Box — AT-6F

Figure 12a — Rear Cockpit Electrical Control Panel
— AT-6F

contained in the engine gage units on the two instrument panels. The oil cooler shutter control in the front cockpit is the only manually operated oil system control and is provided for operation in extreme cold weather only. When the handle is in the up position, the shutters are "CLOSED" and when in the down position, the shutters are "OPEN". The control quadrant is notched to permit setting in any intermediate position.

b. OIL DILUTION SYSTEM.—The oil dilution system is controlled by a switch on the front cockpit electrical control panel. With this switch in the "ON" position, the solenoid valve opens and allows fuel to enter the oil system at the oil "Y" drain valve to lower the viscosity of the oil for cold weather starts.

10. ELECTRICAL SYSTEM.

a. GENERAL.—Twenty-four volt direct current is distributed by single hot wire with the metallic structure of the airplane serving as a return. Power for the electrical system is supplied by a 50-ampere engine-driven generator with 34-ampere-hour storage battery for reserve. An external power receptacle is located on the left lower side of the fuselage. External power should be used instead of the airplane battery to start the engine and operate the electrical system while the airplane is on the ground. Circuit breakers are employed for the protection of all circuits except the generator circuit. They are accessible for resetting from the left side of the front cockpit only. *(See figure 13.)*

b. CONTROLS. *(See figures 11, 11a, 12, and 12a.)*— Controls for all electrical equipment are on the electrical control panel in the front cockpit. Controls for the fluorescent, compass, and fuel gage lights are duplicated in the rear cockpit. Landing light switches are provided on the rear cockpit instrument panel of the AT-6F airplane.

c. LIGHTS—A swivel-mounted cockpit light in each

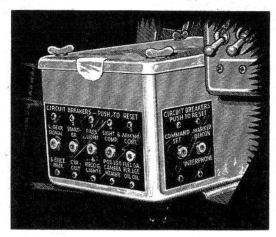

Figure 13 — Circuit Breaker Installation

cockpit is controlled by a rheostat on the light housing.

Fluorescent lamps are installed in each cockpit and are equipped with rotating lens housings to select visible or invisible illumination.

Position light switches provide two intensities— "DIM" and "BRIGHT".

Landing lights and the passing light are individually controlled.

The red, green, and amber recognition lights are individually controlled by switches adjacent to the front cockpit electrical control panel. The "WHITE" switch has no function in this installation.

11. INSTRUMENTS.

(See figures 7, 10, 14 and 15.)

a. PANELS.—A full complement of engine and flight instruments are arranged in the conventional manner in the front panel and sufficient instruments for ordinary flight are in the rear panel on AT-6D models. A standardized arrangement of both panels with flight and engine instruments grouped for easy reference and separated by a yellow border are installed on AT-6F airplanes.

b. FLIGHT INSTRUMENTS.
Air Speed Indicator
Altimeter
Bank and Turn Indicator
Compass, Magnetic
Compass, Remote Reading (Group III airplanes only)
Directional Gyro
Gyro Horizon
Rate of Climb Indicator
These instruments are installed on both instrument panels. The gyro horizon, directional gyro, and bank and turn indicator are gyro instruments run by an engine-driven vacuum pump. The altimeter and climb indicator are connected to the static side of the pitot-static tube. The air indicator is connected to the pressure side of the pitot-static tube. A pitot head heater switch is located on the front cockpit electrical control panel. Each compass incorporates a lamp controlled by a rheostat located on the respective electrical control panel. Compasses on both instrument panels of the AT-6F airplane are lighted by the instrument lights. An accelerometer is installed on some Group I airplanes.

c. ENGINE INSTRUMENTS.
Carburetor Mixture Temperature Gage
Cylinder Head Temperature Gage
Engine Gage Unit (fuel and oil pressure, and oil temperature)
Fuel-Air Ratio Gage (on Groups I and II AT-6D airplanes only)
Manifold Pressure Gage
Tachometer
These instruments are located on the instrument

position, the solenoid valve opens and allows fuel to enter the oil system at the oil "Y" drain valve to lower the viscosity of the oil for cold weather starts.

10. ELECTRICAL SYSTEM.

a. GENERAL.—Twelve-volt direct current is distributed by single hot wire with the metallic structure of the airplane serving as a return. Power for the electrical system is supplied by a 50-ampere engine-driven generator with a 68-ampere-hour storage battery for reserve. Fluorescent and compass lights requiring alternating current are supplied by a d-c to a-c inverter. All circuits except the bomb release and gun firing circuits are fused in the main fuse box at the left side of the front cockpit.

b. CONTROLS. *(See figures 11 and 12.)*—Controls for all electrical equipment are on the electrical control panel in the front cockpit. Controls for the fluorescent, compass, and fuel gage lights are duplicated in the rear cockpit.

c. LIGHTS.—Two swivel-mounted cockpit lights in each cockpit are controlled by a rheostat on the light housing.

A fluorescent lamp is installed on a flexible cable in each cockpit to illuminate the instrument panel.

Position light switches provide two intensities— "DIM" and "BRIGHT".

Landing lights and the passing light are individually controlled.

The red, green, and amber recognition lights are individually controlled by switches adjacent to the front cockpit electrical control panel. The "WHITE" switch has no function in this installation.

11. INSTRUMENTS.

(See figures 7 and 10.)

a. FLIGHT INSTRUMENTS.

Figure 13 – Starter Switch Pedal

Accelerometer
Air Speed Indicator
Altimeter
Bank and Turn Indicator
Compass, Magnetic
Directional Gyro
Gyro Horizon
Rate of Climb Indicator

These instruments, except the accelerometer which is installed in the front cockpit only, are provided on both instrument panels. The gyro horizon, directional gyro, and bank and turn indicator are gyro instruments run by an engine-driven vacuum pump. The altimeter, rate of climb indicator, and air speed indicator are connected to the pitot head. A pitot head heater switch is located on the front cockpit electrical control panel. Each compass incorporates a lamp controlled by a rheostat located on the respective electrical control panel.

b. ENGINE INSTRUMENTS.

Carburetor Mixture Gage
Cylinder Head Temperature Gage
Engine Gage Unit (fuel and oil pressure, and oil temperature)
Fuel-Air Ratio Gage (on early SNJ-4 and all AT-6C airplanes)
Manifold Pressure Gage
Tachometer

These instruments are located on the instrument panel in the front cockpit. The engine gage unit and tachometer are duplicated on the rear cockpit instrument panel.

c. MISCELLANEOUS INSTRUMENTS.

Ammeter
Clock
Free-Air Temperature Indicator
Suction Gage
Voltmeter

The clock and suction gage are installed on both instrument panels. The free-air temperature indicator is installed on the front instrument panel only. The ammeter and voltmeter are located on the front cockpit electrical control panel.

12. HEATING AND VENTILATING SYSTEMS.

Ventilating controls are provided between the rudder pedals in the front cockpit. The volume of hot air taken from the exhaust shroud or cold air from an outside opening is regulated by operating a notched control wheel fitted with a butterfly valve at the outlet of each system. A ventilator door is located at the left rear side of the rear cockpit. A handle located directly beneath the fire extinguisher controls the flow of air.

Airplanes allocated to the United Kingdom contain

a special heating system to heat both cockpits and the wing gun and to defrost the windshield. A control valve is operated by a handle located on the right side of the front cockpit.

13. MISCELLANEOUS EQUIPMENT.

a. PILOT'S RELIEF TUBE.—A relief tube horn is attached by a bracket to the bottom of each seat.

b. ENGINE CRANK.—An engine crank is stowed at the rear of the baggage compartment.

c. INSTRUMENT FLYING HOOD. *(See figure 29.)* —Provisions are included in each cockpit for the installation and operation of an instrument flying hood.

d. DATA AND MAP CASES.—A flight report case is provided at the left side of each cockpit seat and a map and data case is mounted below the radio equipment in the front cockpit.

SECTION II
NORMAL OPERATING INSTRUCTIONS

1. BEFORE ENTERING THE PILOT'S COCKPIT.

a. FLIGHT LIMITATIONS AND RESTRICTIONS.

(1) MANEUVERS PROHIBITED.
Outside loop
Inverted flight in excess of 10 seconds
Snap rolls in excess of 130 IAS
Slow rolls in excess of 190 IAS
Spins and stalls when normal gross weight is exceeded

WARNING

Solo flights should never be made in the rear cockpit.

(2) AIR SPEED LIMITATIONS.
Maximum permissible diving speed is 251 IAS.
With wing flaps set at 45 degrees, do not exceed 125 IAS.
In a sideslip, stay above 90 IAS.
Do not lower landing gear above 150 IAS.

Note

These limitations may be supplemented or superseded by instructions included in Service publications.

b. DATA CHECK.

(1) Make sure the airplane has been serviced and is ready for flight. Check Form 1.

(2) Check Weight and Balance Charts in the data case to ascertain that the load and balance requirements of the airplane are satisfied.

c. ENTRY.—To gain entrance to either cockpit, lift the latch and push the sliding enclosure.

2. ON ENTERING THE PILOT'S COCKPIT.

a. STANDARD CHECK FOR ALL FLIGHTS.

(1) Adjust rudder pedals for proper leg length to obtain full brake control while taxying. *(See figure 15.)*

(2) Adjust the seat level to obtain full rudder travel. *(See figure 16.)*

(3) See that ignition switch *(33 figure 7)* is "OFF".

(4) Set parking brakes *(61 figure 7)*.

(5) Check that all armament switches are "OFF". *(See figure 11.)*

Figure 14 - Instrument Marking - Replaced by Chart on Page 24A.

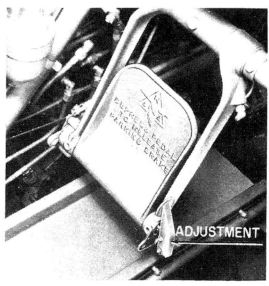

Figure 15 — Rudder Pedal and Adjustment

(6) See that landing gear control handle *(4 figure 5)* is in the "DOWN" position.

(7) Unlock the surface control lock. *(See figure 17.)*

(8) Set altimeter *(36 figure 7)* to correct barometric pressure.

(9) Place battery-disconnect switch in "ON" position. *(See figure 11.)*

(10) Check gun sight illumination by placing "GUN SIGHT" rheostat in "ON" position. *(See figure 11.)*

(11) Check pitot head heater by placing "PITOT HEAT" switch in "ON" position momentarily. *(See figure 11.)*

CAUTION

If pitot head heater is left on for relatively long periods on the ground, the element may be damaged or burned out.

(12) If use of interphone equipment is desired, check the system for proper functioning. For operating instructions, see section V.

(13) Check fuel pressure warning light by operating test switch. *(See figure 11.)*

(14) If oxygen is to be used, check for satisfactory operation. Check gage for pressure above 1800 lb/sq in.

b. SPECIAL CHECK FOR NIGHT FLIGHTS.—*(See figure 11.)*

(1) Turn "ON" desired cockpit and instrument lights.

(2) Turn "ON" the fuel gage lights.

(3) Turn "ON" compass lights.

(4) Turn position lights to "DIM" and "BRIGHT".

(5) Check operation of landing lights and passing light.

(6) Check operation of recognition lights.

CAUTION

Do not operate recognition, passing, or landing lights for more than 10 seconds when the airplane is on the ground, as there must be air circulation to dissipate the heat from the light.

3. FUEL AND OIL SYSTEM MANAGEMENT.

a. Check fuel selector valve *(6 figure 5)* operation before take-off. The following fuel selector valve positions are recommended:

Start	"RESERVE"
Warm-up	Check all tanks
Taxying and take-off	"RESERVE"
Cruise	"LEFT" and "RIGHT" to maintain trim
Acrobatics	"RESERVE"
Landing	"RESERVE"

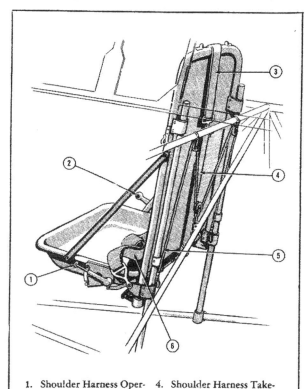

1. Shoulder Harness Operating Lever
2. Elevation Lock Handle
3. Shoulder Harness
4. Shoulder Harness Take-Up Mechanism
5. Shock Cord
6. Safety Belt

Figure 16 — Pilot Seat

Figure 17 — Surface Control Lock

b. Oil dilution is accomplished in the following manner:

(1) Operate the engine at 1000 to 1200 rpm.

(2) Maintain oil temperature from 5° to 50°C and oil pressure above 15 lb/sq in.

(3) Dilute engine oil as follows for ground temperatures shown: (The oil dilution switch must be held "ON".) *(See figure 11.)*

<pre>
4° to −12°C (40° to +10°F) 3 minutes
−12° to −29°C (10° to −20°F) 6 minutes
−29° to −46°C (−20° to −50°F) 9 minutes
Add 1 minute of dilution for each additional
5°C (9°F) below −46°C.
</pre>

(4) During the last minute of dilution, increase rpm to 1500 and slowly move the throttle *(1 figure 21)* to give 26 in. Hg and then back to the original position.

4. STARTING ENGINE.

a. Head the airplane into the wind and set the parking brakes.

b. If flying solo, make certain that the rear cockpit stick is locked in the *stowed* position. See that there is no equipment in the rear cockpit that might foul the controls.

c. Visually check that fire guard is posted.

d. See that ignition switch is "OFF".

e. Have ground personnel turn propeller **6 blades** by hand.

f. Open throttle *(1 figure 21)* approximately ½ inch (600-800 rpm).

g. Move mixture control *(3 figure 21)* to full "RICH".

h. Propeller control *(5 figure 21)* in full "DECREASE RPM".

i. Place carburetor heat control *(7 figure 5)* to full "COLD".

j. Ascertain that the oil cooler shutters *(60 figure 7)* are "OPEN".

k. Turn fuel selector to "RESERVE". *(See figure 18.)*

l. Turn battery and generator main line switches "ON". *(See figure 11.)*

CAUTION
Use hand crank for all cold weather starts.

m. Turn ignition switch *(33 figure 7)* to "BOTH".

n. Prime engine four to six strokes when cold, two to four strokes when warm, and none when hot. *(See 57 figure 7.)*

o. Check to see that propeller is clear.

WARNING
Use of hand fuel pump may flood carburetor with subsequent fire hazard.

q. Press heel of starter pedal. *(See figure 13.)* When the flywheel has reached maximum rpm, engage the starter with the engine by pressing the toe of the starter pedal. As the engine starts, release pressure on the pedal.

WARNING
If a fire develops due to backfiring, it can be extinguished by immediately re-energizing and re-engaging the starter.

r. After the engine has fired, manipulate the throttle to obtain 500 to 600 rpm as quickly as possible.

s. Check the oil pressure. If oil pressure gage registers no pressure after 30 seconds, stop the engine and investigate.

Figure 18 — Fuel Selector Control

5. WARM-UP AND GROUND TEST.

a. When oil pressure reaches 70 to 90 lb/sq in., open the throttle *(1 figure 21)* to obtain approximately 1000 rpm.

b. Set propeller control at full "INCREASE RPM".

c. Check instruments for the following limitations:

	DESIRED	MINIMUM	MAXIMUM
Oil Pressure	70-90	50	100
Oil Temperature	60°C to 80°C	40°C	95°C
Fuel Pressure	3-4	3	4

d. Check reserve, left, and right fuel systems by rotating fuel selector *(6 figure 5)*.

e. Open manifold pressure gage drain *(12 figure 5)* momentarily.

f. With Propeller control in full "INCREASE RPM", move throttle forward to obtain 1800 rpm. Check "L" and "R" magnetos. A maximum loss of 100 rpm is permissible in switching from both magnetos to one.

Note

Always return ignition switch to "BOTH" to allow engine to pick up lost rpm before checking the other magneto.

g. At 700 rpm, check "OFF" position of ignition switch.

b. At 1000 rpm, check the following:

Suction	3.75 to 4.25 in. Hg
Hydraulic Pressure	800 to 1000 lb/sq in.
	(power control lever engaged)
Ammeter	50 amps maximum

i. Check to determine that generator cuts in for charging between 1000 and 1200 rpm by checking voltmeter and ammeter. *(See figure 11.)* Voltmeter should register between 14.25 and 14.5 volts. Charging rate as indicated by the ammeter depends on the condition of the battery.

j. At 1600 rpm, move propeller control *(5 figure 21)* back to note 200 rpm drop (maximum); then move forward to full "INCREASE RPM".

k. Check operation of wing flaps with hand pump *(5 figure 5)* and engine-driven hydraulic pump.

CAUTION

Avoid prolonged operation above 1400 rpm. Do not exceed 232°C (450°F) cylinder head temperature during ground operations.

l. Check flying controls for free movement. Look at control surfaces.

Figure 19 -- Fuel Contents Gages

m. Set the elevator and rudder trim tabs *(8 and 9 figure 5)* at "NEUTRAL".

n. Check communication equipment for proper operation. (See section V, paragraph 1.)

o. Release parking brakes.

6. SCRAMBLE TAKE-OFF.

Use oil dilution (2 minutes maximum) to obtain proper oil pressure at moderate power. Check for a rise in oil temperature, and as soon as the engine will *take* the throttle, release the parking brakes, taxi out, and take off.

7. TAXYING INSTRUCTIONS.

a. Steer a zigzag course to obtain an unobstructed view.

b. Use the brakes as little as possible and always taxi cautiously.

c. Upon reaching the take-off position, stop the airplane cross-wind so approaching airplanes may be seen plainly.

d. If take-off is delayed, clear the engine by opening the throttle against the brakes to about 25 in. Hg manifold pressure (1900 rpm).

8. TAKE-OFF.

a. When take-off area is clear, quickly check the following:

(1) Generator main line switch "ON"

(2) Mixture control full "RICH"

(3) Fuel selector on "RESERVE" (Check fuel levels.)

(4) Fuel pressure 3 to 4 lb/sq in.

(5) Propeller control full "INCREASE RPM"

(6) Carburetor air control in full "COLD"

(7) Wing flaps "UP" (If high obstacles are to be cleared and only a short run is available, place flaps in 15 degrees down.)

(8) Gyro instruments uncaged

Note

Gyro instruments should be left uncaged at all times except during acrobatics. When the rear cockpit is unoccupied, cage the rear gyro instruments before take-off.

(9) Oil pressure 70 to 90 lb/sq in.

(10) Oil temperature 50° to 70°C.

(11) Cylinder head temperature 150°C minimum for take-off.

b. Adjust throttle friction sufficiently to prevent creepage if hand is removed.

c. Check lap belt, tighten and lock shoulder harness.

d. Turn into the wind and open throttle gradually (3 to 5 seconds desirable) to 36 in. Hg and take off at 2250 rpm (maximum cylinder head temperature 260°C

(500°F) for 5 minutes).

e. Do not attempt to lift the tail too soon, as this increases the torque action. Maintain a constant attitude until sufficient speed is attained, then raise the tail slowly.

9. ENGINE FAILURE DURING TAKE-OFF.

a. To reduce the possibility of and danger from engine failure during take-off, observe the following practices:

(1) Run up engine carefully and check thoroughly before take-off.

(2) Retract the landing gear as soon as the airplane is definitely air-borne.

(3) If flaps are used, raise as soon as the airplane reaches a safe altitude.

b. If the engine fails immediately after take-off:

(1) Depress the nose at once so that the air speed does not drop below stalling speed.

(2) If bombs are installed, salvo them immediately.

(3) Open the sliding enclosure.

(4) If the landing gear has started to come up, *do not try to lower it.*

(5) Lower the flaps fully if possible.

(6) Turn "OFF" ignition switch and battery disconnect switch.

(7) Turn fuel selector valve "OFF".

(8) Land straight ahead, changing direction only to miss obstructions.

10. CLIMB.

As soon as the airplane is sufficiently clear of the ground, proceed as follows:

a. Push the hydraulic power control lever *(1 figure 5)*.

b. Retract the landing gear. Pull the landing gear control *(4 figure 5)* to the "UP" position and leave it up.

c. Ease back on the throttle to 32.5 in. Hg and propeller control to about 2200 rpm. Climb at 115 rpm IAS.

d. Raise the flaps if used. Pull the flap control *(2 figure 5)* to the "UP" position and leave it up.

CAUTION

Always reduce manifold pressure first, then rpm. Move throttle and propeller controls slowly.

e. Check the cylinder head and oil temperatures and the oil pressure.

f. Turn the fuel selector from "RESERVE" to "LEFT". (See figure 18.)

g. Adjust the trim tabs *(8 and 9 figure 5)* so that airplane flies *hands off*.

h. Refer to "Take-Off, Climb, and Landing Chart", appendix I, for rates of climb applicable.

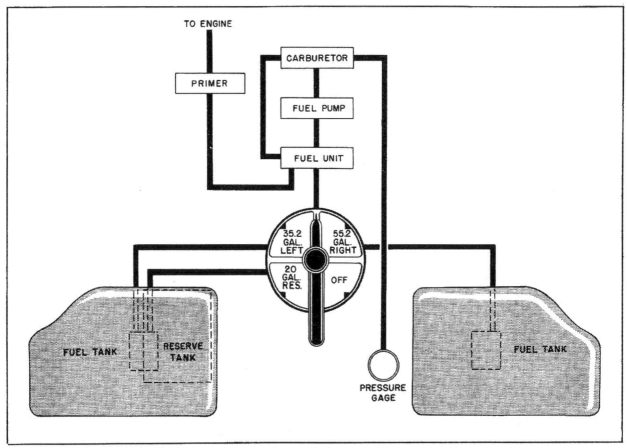

Figure 20 — Fuel Flow Diagram

11. GENERAL FLYING CHARACTERISTICS.

a. The lowest fuel consumption is obtained by using a lean mixture and throttling down the engine to the lowest speed at which the airplane will fly satisfactorily and the engine will run smoothly. This speed is 130 mph at 1600 rpm and 24 in. Hg, the propeller in "DE-CREASE RPM", at approximately 1000 feet altitude.

b. Although less economical, the desired cruising conditions are 1850 rpm, 26 in. Hg, and 155 mph at 5,000 feet altitude. Do not lean the mixture too much, as serious damage may result from overheated cylinders.

c. For engine operation, refer to "Power Plant Chart", section III, and "Flight Operation Instruction Charts", appendix I.

d. The effect of flap and landing gear operation on the trim of the airplane in flight is as follows:

Landing gear retracted .... no effect
Landing gear extended .... no effect
Flaps lowered .... nose heavy
Flaps raised .... tail heavy
Flaps raised from
full down at 80 IAS .... airplane sinks
                                       approximately 20 feet
Flaps raised from
full down at 75 IAS .... airplane sinks
                                       approximately 40 feet

e. Air speed must not fall below 90 IAS while sideslipping. Recovery from a sideslip should be effected above 200 feet.

f. Surface controls, particularly the rudder, are slightly less responsive with the flaps down; therefore turns and sideslips with the flaps fully lowered must not be made with less than 400 feet altitude.

g. Runaway propeller caused by excess power and decreased load on the engine, present in a prolonged steep dive, should be corrected by reducing the throttle setting and returning the airplane to normal flight attitude. During such dives, keep manifold pressure above 15 in. Hg, pay careful attention to tachometer readings, and reduce the throttle as necessary to prevent increased engine speed. A quick increase in throttle setting after the throttle has been retarded, with propeller control set for 1900 rpm, can also cause a runaway propeller. This change in rpm usually occurs at the critical period following take-off or in approach for landing when the throttle is momentarily decreased to check operation of the landing gear warning horn, at which time little excess altitude is available for emergencies. This rapid increase may cause the engine to overspeed which destroys the sensitive balance of constant speed control. To remedy, immediately put an increased load upon the ting and returning the airplane to normal flight attitude. During such dives, keep manifold pressure above 15 in. Hg, pay careful attention to tachometer readings, and reduce the throttle as necessary to prevent increased engine speed. A quick increase in throttle setting after the throttle has been retarded, with propeller control set for 1900 rpm, can also cause a runaway propeller. This change in rpm usually occurs at the critical period following take-off or in approach for landing when the throttle is momentarily decreased to check operation of the landing gear warning horn, at which time little excess altitude is available for emergencies. This rapid increase may cause the engine to overspeed which destroys the sensitive balance of constant speed control. To remedy, immediately put an increased load upon the engine and propeller by putting the airplane in a climbing attitude, if possible, and slowly retard the throttle setting until the rpm again comes under control.

b. Gliding may be carried out at any safe speed down to the recommended margin of about 25 percent above stalling speed. With the landing gear and flaps up the glide is very flat, and at the best gliding speed of about 100 rpm IAS, long distances can be covered for a comparatively small loss of altitude. Lowering either flaps or landing gear greatly steepens the gliding angle and increases the rate of descent.

GLIDING SPEED CHART

IAS	GLIDING ANGLE	L. G. and FLAPS	POWER
100	Best	"UP"	"OFF"
95	Best	"DOWN"	"OFF"
90	Steep	"DOWN"	"OFF"
85	Best	"DOWN"	"ON"
80	Steep	"DOWN"	"ON"

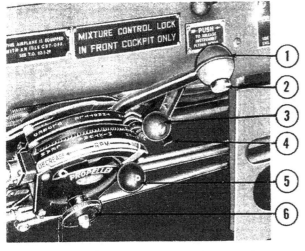

1. Throttle Control   4. Mixture Control Lock Release
2. Throat Microphone Switch   5. Propeller Control
3. Mixture Control   6. Friction Lock

Figure 21 — Engine Control Quadrant — Front Cockpit

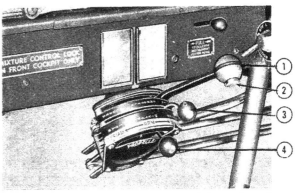

1. Throttle Control   3. Mixture Control
2. Throat Microphone Switch   4. Propeller Control

Figure 22 — Engine Control Quadrant — Rear Cockpit

12. STALLS.

STALLING SPEED CHART

GROSS WEIGHT	GEAR AND FLAPS UP	GEAR AND FLAPS DOWN
5300 Pounds	72 mph (IAS)	64 mph (IAS)
6000 Pounds	77 mph (IAS)	69 mph (IAS)

a. When the stalling incidence is reached with landing gear and flaps up, a wing will drop. If the backward movement on the stick continues when the wing drops, the airplane will fall into a steep spiral. The stalling incidence is reached with the control stick only a short distance back when the airplane nears stalling speed, because of sensitive elevators.

b. Decrease the whip when stalling by putting the stick forward at the start and applying opposite rudder. If putting the stick forward is delayed until the airplane is on its back, an inverted spin may result.

c. No warning of a stall should be relied on, although buffeting and pitching usually precede a stall.

d. During a practice stall, do not pull the nose up in order to stall; instead, counteract its tendency to sink by easing back the stick. When a wing drops, put the stick forward at once and apply opposite rudder.

e. With flaps and landing gear down, stalling incidence is reached about 64 mph IAS. As speed is reduced, the right wing drops quickly and; unless recovery is effected immediately, the airplane may whip into a half roll and attempt to spin.

13. SPINS.

Spins should not be made intentionally with flaps and landing gear down. Should an inadvertent spin occur, recovery can be effected after 1-1/2 or 2 turns by first applying full opposite rudder and then pushing the control stick forward to neutral. The ailerons are held in the neutral position. Centralize the rudder as soon as the airplane is in a straight dive to prevent a spin in the opposite direction. Bring the airplane out of the dive and return the control stick to neutral.

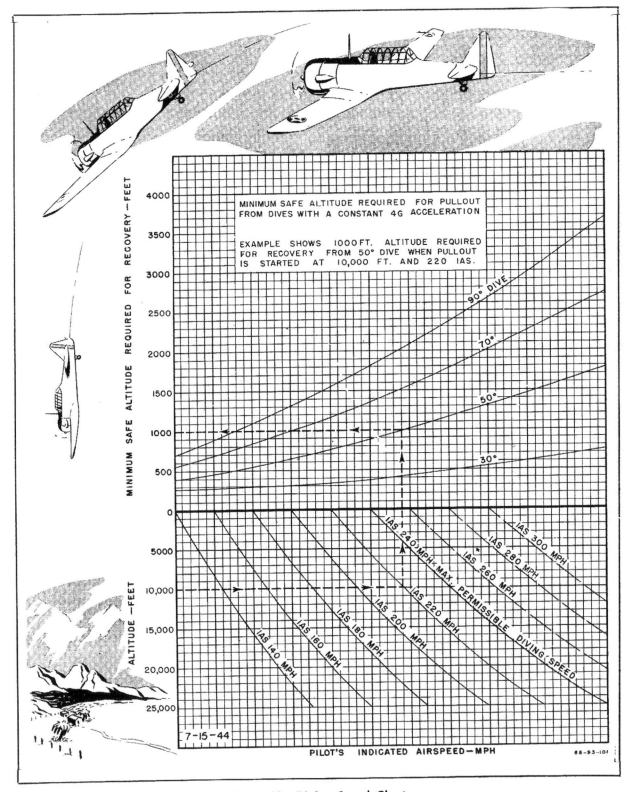

Figure 23 — Diving Speed Chart

14. PERMISSIBLE ACROBATICS.

The acrobatic qualities of this airplane are exceptional, and the lateral control is excellent at all speeds. All normal acrobatics except those prohibited in paragraph 1 of this section are permitted; however, inverted flying must be limited to 10 seconds because of engine difficulties resulting from prolonged inverted flight.

15. DIVING.

(See figure 23.)

The maximum permissible diving speed is 240 IAS, during which the engine speed must not exceed 2800 rpm and 20 in. Hg with the throttle open 1/3 or more. However, with the throttle closed, 2200 rpm is the maximum allowable to keep engine stresses down. The propeller must be in the "DECREASE RPM" position in a dive. Move the control to "DECREASE RPM" while the throttle is still partially open to prevent the propeller blades from remaining set in "INCREASE RPM" during the dive. The use of elevator tabs is not required for dive recovery.

16. NIGHT FLYING.

The sequence outlined for daylight operation should be observed even more strictly for night flights. In addition, the pilot should familiarize himself with the location of the different lights and their switches.

17. APPROACH AND LANDING.

(See figure 24.)

a. APPROACH.—When the airplane approaches the field, adhere to the following sequence of operation:

(1) Place fuel selector on "RESERVE". *(See figure 18.)*

(2) Set mixture control *(3 figure 21)* in full "RICH".

(3) Set propeller control *(5 figure 21)* in the maximum cruising rpm position (2000 rpm).

(4) Reduce speed to less than 150 IAS.

(5) Press the power control lever *(1 figure 5)*.

(6) Lower the landing gear by placing the landing gear control *(4 figure 5)* in the "DOWN" position. Leave the control in the "DOWN" position.

(7) Reduce speed to less than 126 IAS.

(8) Lower the flaps as needed, on final approach after turn into field has been made, and between 90 and 95 IAS. Flaps are lowered by placing the flap control *(2 figure 5)* in the "DOWN" position and leaving it there.

b. LANDING.

(1) GENERAL.—Having turned into the field and lowered the flaps, adjust the rudder and elevator trim tabs *(8 figure 5)* to maintain a correct gliding speed. Having stopped after landing, raise the flaps before taxying.

(2) CROSS-WIND LANDING.—As this airplane has a landing gear of wide tread, cross-wind landings may be negotiated safely. Keep one wing down, into the wind, to counteract drift.

(3) TAKE-OFF IF LANDING IS NOT COMPLETED.—In the event of an unsuccessful attempt to land, open the throttle and take off. Raise the landing gear immediately; then, when the air speed has reached

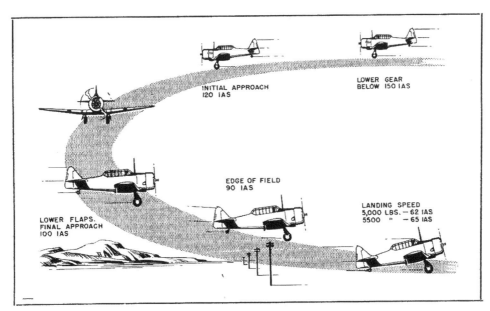

Figure 24 — Landing Diagram

100 MPH IAS and with an altitude of at least 300 feet, raise the flaps *(2 figure 5)*.

18. STOPPING OF ENGINE.

a. If a cold weather start is anticipated, dilute the engine oil as outlined in paragraph 3 of this section.

b. Open the throttle to about 1200 rpm and put propeller control *(5 figure 21)* at "DECREASE RPM"; allow engine to run for one minute.

c. Place mixture control *(3 figure 21)* in full "LEAN", making use of idle cut-off.

d. Place throttle *(1 figure 21)* in full "OPEN".

e. Turn ignition switch *(33 figure 7)* "OFF" after engine ceases firing.

f. Turn fuel selector "OFF". *(See figure 18.)*

19. BEFORE LEAVING COCKPIT.

After engine stops, proceed as follows:

a. Turn "OFF" all switches.

b. Move throttle to "CLOSED".

c. Lock the surface controls. *(See figure 17.)*

d. Apply parking brakes *(61 figure 7)* when brakes have cooled sufficiently.

20. MOORING.

(See figure 25.)

a. Head the airplane into the wind.

b. Set parking brakes.

c. Lock the surface controls.

d. Insert the mooring rings in the wings. Moor the airplane to ground mooring rings or sandbags with ¾-inch rope or ¼-inch cable. Secure the tail at the lift-mooring tube or by lashing directly to the tail wheel fork.

e. Install covers.

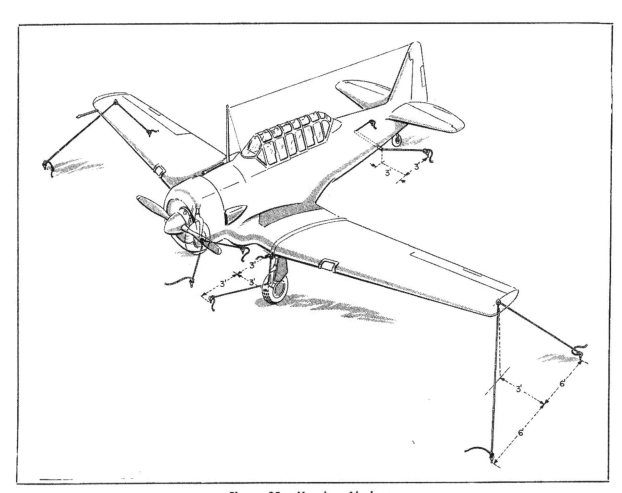

Figure 25 — Mooring Airplane

SECTION III
FLIGHT OPERATING DATA

1. POWER PLANT CHART.

a. Operating limitations and characteristics of the R-1340-AN-1 engine are summarized on the "Power Plant Chart". The pilot should be thoroughly familiar with this information.

b. Engine operating conditions shown on the chart are defined as follows:

(1) WAR EMERGENCY.—Not applicable.

(2) MILITARY POWER. — Maximum recommended for operation for periods not exceeding 5 minutes.

(3) NORMAL RATED.—Maximum recommended for operation with rich mixture in climb and level flight.

(4) MAXIMUM CRUISE. — Maximum recommended with lean mixture.

(5) TAKE-OFF CONDITIONS. — Maximum recommended for take-off under the specified time limit of 5 minutes.

2. AIR SPEED LIMITATIONS.

Refer to section II, paragraph 1.

3. AIR SPEED CORRECTION TABLE.

IAS	IAS CALI-BRATED	ALTIMETER ERROR ADD TO INSTRUMENT READING	
		S. L.	15,000
80	80	0	0
100	101	10	10
120	122.5	20	30
140	144	40	60
160	165.5	60	100
180	187	90	140
200	208.5	120	190

POWER PLANT CHART

AIRCRAFT MODEL(S)	PROPELLER(S)	ENGINE MODEL(S)
AT-6 SNJ	12D40	R-1340-AN-1

GAUGE READING	FUEL PRESS.	OIL PRESS.	OIL TEMP.	COOLANT TEMP.		OIL(1) CONS.
DESIRED MAXIMUM	3-5	50-70 100	70 95			7.5
MINIMUM IDLING	3 2	50 15				

MAXIMUM PERMISSIBLE DIVING RPM: 2800
MINIMUM RECOMMENDED CRUISE RPM: 1600
MAXIMUM RECOMMENDED TURBO RPM:

OIL GRADE: (S) 1120 (W) 1100
FUEL GRADE: 87 SPEC. AN-F-25

WAR EMERGENCY (COMBAT EMERGENCY)			MILITARY POWER (NON-COMBAT EMERGENCY)			OPERATING CONDITION			NORMAL RATED (MAXIMUM CONTINUOUS)			MAXIMUM CRUISE (NORMAL OPERATION)		
MINUTES			5 MINUTES 260°C			TIME LIMIT MAX. CYL. HD. TEMP.			UNLIMITED 260°C			UNLIMITED 232°C		
			RICH 2250			MIXTURE R. P. M.			RICH 2200			LEAN 2000		
MANIF. PRESS.	SUPER-CHARGER	FUEL(2) Gal/Min	MANIF. PRESS.	SUPER-CHARGER	FUEL(2) Gal/Min	STD. TEMP. °C	PRESSURE ALTITUDE	STD. TEMP. °F	MANIF. PRESS.	SUPER-CHARGER	FUEL GPH(3)	MANIF. PRESS.	SUPER-CHARGER	FUEL GPH(3)
						-55.0 -55.0 -55.0	40,000 FT. 38,000 FT. 36,000 FT.	-67.0 -67.0 -67.0						
						-52.4 -48.4 -44.4	34,000 FT. 32,000 FT. 30,000 FT.	-62.3 -55.1 -48.0						
						-40.5 -36.5 -32.5	28,000 FT. 26,000 FT. 24,000 FT.	-40.9 -33.7 -26.5						
			F.T. F.T.		.5 .5	-28.6 -24.6 -20.7	22,000 FT. 20,000 FT. 18,000 FT.	-19.4 -12.3 - 5.2	F.T. F.T.		33 35	F.T. F.T.		25 27
			F.T. F.T. F.T.		.5 .5 1.0	-16.7 -12.7 - 8.8	16,000 FT. 14,000 FT. 12,000 FT.	2.0 9.1 16.2	F.T. F.T. F.T.		37 40 43	F.T. F.T. F.T.		29 31 33
			F.T. F.T. F.T.		1.0 1.0 1.0	- 4.8 - 0.8 3.1	10,000 FT. 8,000 FT. 6,000 FT.	23.4 30.5 37.6	F.T. F.T. F.T.		46 49 53	26.0 26.5 27.5		35 35 34
			F.T. 35.0 36.0		1.0 1.0 1.0	7.1 11.0 15.0	4,000 FT. 2,000 FT. SEA LEVEL	44.7 51.8 59.0	32.5 32.5 32.5		54 52 49	28.5 29.0 30.0		34 34 34

GENERAL NOTES

(1) OIL CONSUMPTION: MAXIMUM U.S. QUART PER HOUR PER ENGINE.
(2) Gal/Min: APPROXIMATE U.S. GALLON PER MINUTE PER ENGINE.
(3) GPH: APPROXIMATE U.S. GALLON PER HOUR PER ENGINE.
   F.T.: MEANS FULL THROTTLE OPERATION.
   VALUES ARE FOR LEVEL FLIGHT WITH RAM.

FOR COMPLETE CRUISING DATA SEE APPENDIX II
NOTE: TO DETERMINE CONSUMPTION IN BRITISH
IMPERIAL UNITS, MULTIPLY BY 10 THEN DIVIDE
BY 12. RED FIGURES ARE PRELIMINARY SUBJECT
TO REVISION AFTER FLIGHT CHECK.

TAKE-OFF CONDITIONS:	CONDITIONS TO AVOID:
2250 RPM AND 36" HG	OPERATION BELOW 1500 RPM

SPECIAL NOTES

1. THE MIXTURE CONTROL IN THIS AIRPLANE IS NOT AUTOMATIC
   AND MUST BE ADJUSTED MANUALLY TO OBTAIN SMOOTH ENGINE
   OPERATION AND BEST RANGE.

AAFMC-526
8-1-05

DATA AS OF 8-10-44 BASED ON FLIGHT TESTS

Figure 26 — Power Plant Chart

INSTRUMENT MARKINGS

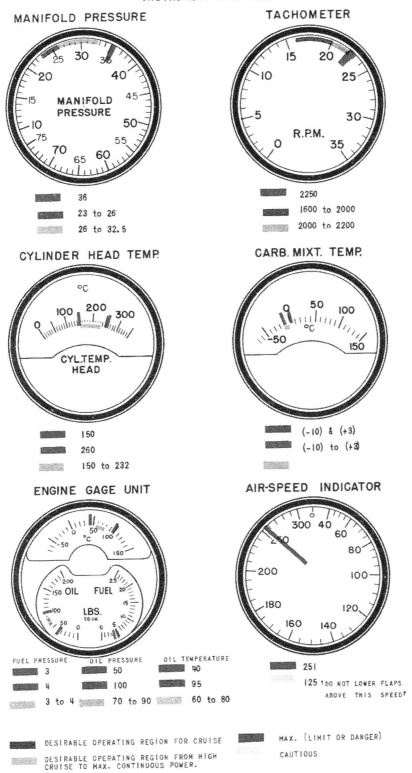

MANIFOLD PRESSURE

TACHOMETER

36	
23 to 26	
26 to 32.5	

2250	
1600 to 2000	
2000 to 2200	

CYLINDER HEAD TEMP.

CARB. MIXT. TEMP.

150	
260	
150 to 232	

(-10) & (+3)	
(-10) to (+3)	

ENGINE GAGE UNIT

AIR-SPEED INDICATOR

FUEL PRESSURE   OIL PRESSURE   OIL TEMPERATURE

3	50	40
4	100	95
3 to 4	70 to 90	60 to 80

251

125 (DO NOT LOWER FLAPS ABOVE THIS SPEED)

DESIRABLE OPERATING REGION FOR CRUISE

MAX. (LIMIT OR DANGER)

DESIRABLE OPERATING REGION FROM HIGH CRUISE TO MAX. CONTINUOUS POWER.

CAUTIOUS

SECTION IV
EMERGENCY OPERATING INSTRUCTIONS

1. GENERAL.

Emergency instructions have been assembled in this section to facilitate quick reference. The pilot should acquaint himself with these instructions before his first flight in this airplane.

2. SCRAMBLE TAKE-OFF

Refer to section II paragraph 6.

3. ENGINE FAILURE DURING TAKE-OFF.

Refer to section II, paragraph 9.

4. ENGINE FAILURE DURING FLIGHT.

If the engine fails during flight, the airplane may be abandoned, ditched, or brought in for a dead-stick landing. Maintain speed by depressing the nose at once, if necessary, so that the air speed does not drop below 95 IAS. Place propeller control in "DECREASE RPM" to reduce drag. Do not attempt sideslips or "S" turns below 2000 feet altitude. Lowering of the flaps may be de-

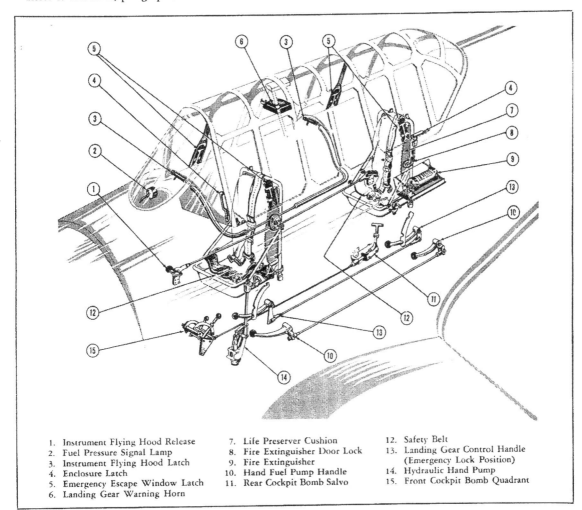

1. Instrument Flying Hood Release
2. Fuel Pressure Signal Lamp
3. Instrument Flying Hood Latch
4. Enclosure Latch
5. Emergency Escape Window Latch
6. Landing Gear Warning Horn
7. Life Preserver Cushion
8. Fire Extinguisher Door Lock
9. Fire Extinguisher
10. Hand Fuel Pump Handle
11. Rear Cockpit Bomb Salvo
12. Safety Belt
13. Landing Gear Control Handle (Emergency Lock Position)
14. Hydraulic Hand Pump
15. Front Cockpit Bomb Quadrant

Figure 27 — Emergency Provisions

layed until the last 300 or 400 feet, but keep in mind that once lowered, they can not be raised.

5. EMERGENCY EXIT DURING FLIGHT.

In the event that an emergency exit must be made during flight, the following procedures are recommended:

a. ENCLOSURE.—Release the sliding enclosure by pushing the lever on the left side of the section and pushing the enclosure back. Unfasten safety belt and shoulder harness, lower self onto wing and roll off, or roll airplane over on its back and drop out.

b. EMERGENCY ESCAPE WINDOW.—If the enclosure is inoperative, raise the red release lever at the bottom center of any side enclosure panel *(5 figure 27)*, thus breaking the safety wire, and push the panel clear of the airplane. This should permit the enclosure to be opened easily. As a last resort, exit through the side window opening.

c. INSTRUMENT BLIND-FLYING HOOD RELEASE.—The instrument flying hood may be released by the occupant of either cockpit.

(1) To release the hood of the adjoining cockpit, push the control knob *(1 figure 27)* on the forward left side of the cockpit.

(2) To release the occupied cockpit hood, push the same control knob or push the lever extending from the latch assembly *(3 figure 27)* located on the left below the edge of the instrument panel shield.

6. DITCHING.

WARNING

Be sure to ditch while fuel is still available for power.

The airplane should be ditched only as a last resort. On an overwater flight, if trouble arises and the pilot is certain that he will not be able to reach land, he should leave the airplane in flight. However, if it is not possible to maintain sufficient altitude for a successful parachute drop, ditching is the only remaining procedure. The instructions for ditching are as follows:

a. If bombs are installed, "SALVO" them immediately.

b. Lock the cockpit enclosure in the open position.

c. Landing gear "UP"

d. Flap 20 degrees.

e. Make certain that safety belt and shoulder harness are fastened securely, as there is a violent deceleration of the airplane upon final impact.

f. Land fully stalled, tail low, with power if possible. In winds up to 40 MPH land parallel to the swells, in winds over 40 MPH land into the wind.

7. EMERGENCY LANDING.

In the event a forced landing is necessary, proceed as follows:

a. Depress the nose to maintain a minimum of 95 IAS.

b. "SALVO" bombs "UNARMED".

c. Keep landing gear retracted.

d. Check safety belt for security.

e. Use flaps so airplane will glide and land in accustomed manner.

f. Land as nearly upwind as possible.

g. If power is available, use it to level airplane just before ground contact.

h. Turn "OFF" the ignition and battery-disconnect switches and fuel selector valve just before landing.

i. Immediately after landing, get clear of airplane.

8. EMERGENCY LOWERING OF FLAPS AND LANDING GEAR.

a. HYDRAULIC HAND PUMP OPERATION.— The hydraulic hand pump *(14 figure 27)* located to the

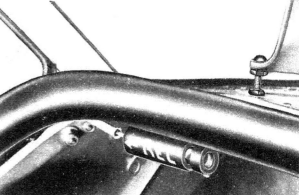

Figure 30 — Instrument Flying Hood Release

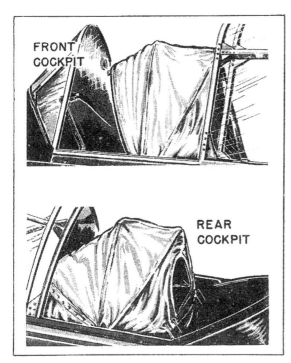

Figure 29 — Instrument Flying Hoods

left of the front cockpit seat is used in event of failure of the engine-driven hydraulic pump. It is not necessary to push the hydraulic power control lever. To operate:

(1) Place the landing gear or flap selector lever in the desired position.

(2) Raise the pump handle to the extended position; turn the pump handle clockwise until it locks, and start pumping.

b. COMPLETE HYDRAULIC FAILURE. — In the event of complete hydraulic system failure, the landing gear may be lowered by placing the landing gear control handle in the "DOWN" position and yawing the airplane. The force of gravity will pull the landing gear to the down position. Place the landing gear control in the "EMERGENCY" locking position *(13 figure 27)* when the indicator shows the gear fully extended. This will mechanically engage the down lockpins. Yaw the airplane again if difficulty in engaging the lockpins is encountered. Flaps cannot be operated in the event of complete hydraulic system failure.

9. ENGINE-DRIVEN FUEL PUMP FAILURE.

Maintain fuel pressure by use of the hand fuel pump *(10 figure 27)* on the control shelf of each cockpit

in the event of engine fuel pump failure. Insufficient operation of the hand pump will be indicated by the fuel pressure warning light *(2 figure 27)*. Maintain 3 to 4 lb/sq in. pressure to supply sufficient fuel to the engine.

10. EMERGENCY BOMB RELEASE.

a. FRONT COCKPIT BOMB QUADRANT.

(1) In order to salvo unarmed, place the bomb safety and nose fuse switches to "SAFE". Move the bomb arming lever of the quadrant to "SAFE". *(See 15 figure 27.)*

(2) Move the release lever to "SALVO".

b. REAR COCKPIT BOMB SALVO. — Pull the emergency salvo handle *(11 figure 27)*. Bombs will drop either "ARMED" or "SAFE", according to the position of the switches on the front cockpit electrical control panel.

11. USE OF MISCELLANEOUS EMERGENCY EQUIPMENT.

a. FIRE EXTINGUISHER.—A carbon tetrachloride hand fire extinguisher is installed on the left side of the rear cockpit. *(See figure 30.)* A hinged door makes it accessible from outside also. To remove, release retaining strap buckle and pull outward. Pressing the red button the left fuselage side panel opens the access door.

b. LIFE PRESERVER.—The back cushion of both cockpit seats is filled with kapok and may be used as a life preserver.

c. PYROTECHNICS.—Provisions are made in early Group I airplanes for stowing a type M-2 pyrotechnic pistol at the right side of the front cockpit. Racks alongside are provided for three type M-10 and three type M-11 signals.

Figure 30 — Fire Extinguisher

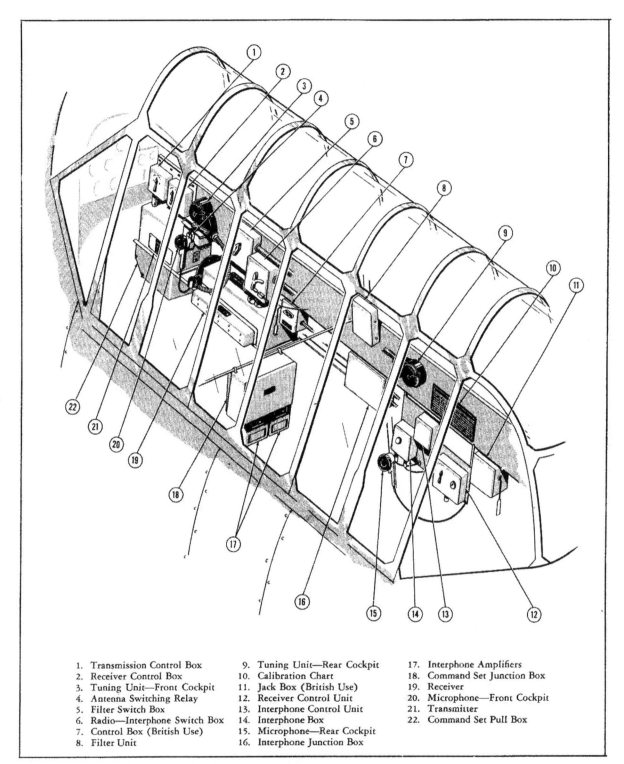

1. Transmission Control Box	9. Tuning Unit—Rear Cockpit	17. Interphone Amplifiers
2. Receiver Control Box	10. Calibration Chart	18. Command Set Junction Box
3. Tuning Unit—Front Cockpit	11. Jack Box (British Use)	19. Receiver
4. Antenna Switching Relay	12. Receiver Control Unit	20. Microphone—Front Cockpit
5. Filter Switch Box	13. Interphone Control Unit	21. Transmitter
6. Radio—Interphone Switch Box	14. Interphone Box	22. Command Set Pull Box
7. Control Box (British Use)	15. Microphone—Rear Cockpit	
8. Filter Unit	16. Interphone Junction Box	

Figure 31 — Communication System

SECTION V
OPERATIONAL EQUIPMENT

1. COMMUNICATION EQUIPMENT.

a. DESCRIPTION. *(See figure 31.)*—The command set SCR-AL-183 installation consists of a transmitter (2500 to 7700 kc) and a receiver (201 to 398 kc and 2500 to 7700 kc), both of which are provided with extra coils and tuning arrangements to obtain the desired operating frequency. Duplicate controls are provided in each cockpit; however choice of reception and type of transmission is controlled from the front cockpit only. An interphone installation, RC-27, provides intercommunication between the two cockpits.

b. OPERATION. — Place the battery-disconnect switch in the "ON" position. To supply power to the communication equipment, place radio control switch *(6 figure 32)* at *"MANUAL"*.

(1) RECEPTION.

(a) Turn radio-interphone switch *(11 figure 32)* to "RADIO".

(b) Plug headphones into "PHONE" jack *(13 figure 32)*.

(c) Wait 45 seconds for receiver to warm. A hum will be heard in the phones.

(d) Turn filter selection switch to "RANGE", "VOICE", or "BOTH", depending on type of reception desired. "BOTH" provides reception of "RANGE" and "VOICE" simultaneously.

(e) Use tuning unit *(8 figure 32)* to tune in desired station.

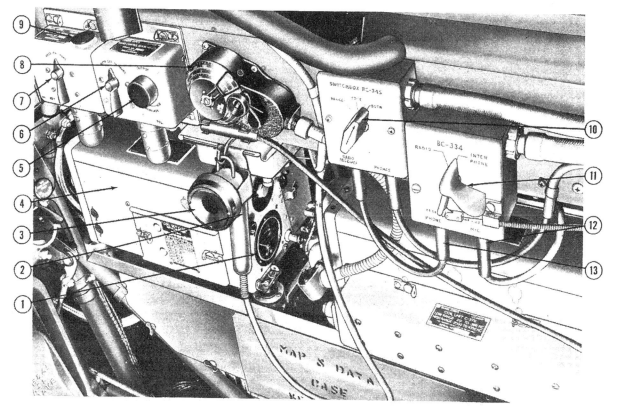

1. Antenna Current Meter	6. Radio Control Switch	10. Filter Selection Switch
2. Microphone Switch	7. Transmitter "VOICE-CW-TONE"	11. Radio-Interphone Switch
3. Microphone	Switch	12. Microphone Jack
4. Radio Transmitter	8. Tuning Unit	13. Head Set Jack
5. Volume Control	9. Telegraph Key	

Figure 32 — Radio Controls — Front Cockpit

1. Interphone Amplifier Switch	4. Tuning Dial	7. Head Set Jack
2. Microphone	5. Radio—Interphone Switch	8. Microphone Jack
3. Tuning Handle	6. Volume Control	9. Microphone Switch

Figure 33 — Radio Controls — Rear Cockpit

f. Use volume control *(5 figure 32)* to obtain desired volume.

(g) Turn control switch from "MANUAL" to "AUTO" for automatic gain control and adjust volume if necessary.

Note

Do not attempt to tune in signals with control switch in "AUTO" position.

(h) To turn off set, turn control switch to "OFF"

(2) TRANSMISSION.

(a) VOICE.

1. Place radio control switch at "MANUAL".

2. Plug microphone into jack marked "MIC." *(12 figure 32).*

3. Turn radio-interphone switch to "RADIO".

4. Turn selector switch to "VOICE".

5. Press microphone switch to talk. A click should be heard in the phones and the antenna circuit meter should register about .8 amperes.

Note

A throat microphone switch is located on each throttle control. Hand microphones are controlled by a switch on each microphone.

(b) KEY.

1. Place radio control switch *(6 figure 32)* at "MANUAL".

2. Turn radio-interphone switch *(11 figure 32)* to "RADIO".

3. Turn selector switch *(7 figure 32)* to "CW" or "TONE", according to the type of transmission desired.

4. Use key *(9 figure 32)* on top of transmitter control unit to send signal.

(3) INTERPHONE.

(a) Make certain the amplifier switch *(1 figure 33)* is "ON".

(b) Place radio-interphone switch to "INTERPHONE" and use microphone as in voice transmission.

c. PREFLIGHT CHECK.

(1) RECEPTION.

(a) Turn the receiver on.

(b) With engine not running, check reception to determine if stations are being received properly.

(c) With engine running check reception for undue electrical interference.

(2) TRANSMISSION.

(a) Set switches for voice transmission.

(b) Call the local control station or other air-

planes operating from the same base for frequency check and to determine if transmission and reception are satisfactory.

d. SIGNAL FAILURES.

(1) BETWEEN AIRPLANES. — Uninterrupted communication between maneuvering airplanes cannot be expected unless they are close together. Best reception is usually obtained with airplanes in level flight. Vertical banks cause minimum signal strength unless both airplanes bank the same direction. A "dead spot" will be present when the receiving airplane is directly above or below the radio mast of the transmitting airplane.

(2) AIRPLANE TO GROUND.—Usually signal fading (rapid variations) is encountered in proportion with the transmission distance; however it may be present at distances of less than 10 miles. Poor quality signals or reception do not necessarily indicate faulty equipment. Make a test at close range before looking for equipment trouble.

e. POST FLIGHT PROCEDURE.

(1) Throw radio control switch *(6 figure 32)* to "OFF".

(2) Throw battery-disconnect switch to "OFF".

(3) Securely fasten all loose equipment, head sets, microphones, etc., in their proper places.

2. BOMBING EQUIPMENT.

a. DESCRIPTION.

(1) GENERAL. *(See figure 34.)*—Complete provisions have been incorporated in the airplane for a flush-type bomb rack and other bombing equipment on the lower surface of each outer wing panel. The bomb racks will carry five M-5, 30-pound fragmentation bombs or five M-41, 20-pound fragmentation bombs, either U.S. or British. Two auxiliary bomb shackles may be added to each of these racks for carrying a total of four Mark I, 100-pound bombs, either U.S. or British, in place of the smaller bombs.

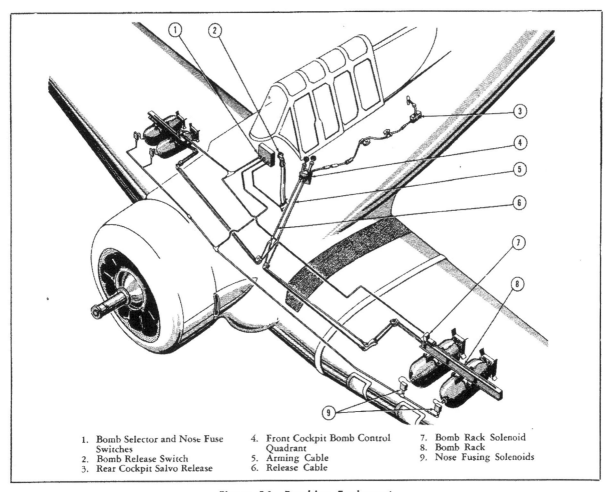

1. Bomb Selector and Nose Fuse Switches	4. Front Cockpit Bomb Control Quadrant	7. Bomb Rack Solenoid
2. Bomb Release Switch	5. Arming Cable	8. Bomb Rack
3. Rear Cockpit Salvo Release	6. Release Cable	9. Nose Fusing Solenoids

Figure 34 — Bombing Equipment

(2) SWITCHES. *(See figure 37.)*—Electrical control switches, which consist of one "BOMB SAFETY" switch, two "BOMB SELECTOR" switches, and one "NOSE FUSE" switch, are grouped on the pilot's electrical control panel in the front cockpit.

(a) The "BOMB SAFETY" switch, when "OFF", prevents accidental electrical release of the bombs. The switch must be "ON" before any electrical release can be accomplished.

(b) The "BOMB SELECTOR" switches provide selection of the rack to be employed. "LEFT" or "RIGHT", or "LEFT" and "RIGHT" can be used as desired.

(c) The "NOSE FUSE" switch operates the four type B-1 bomb arming units to nose-arm the 100-pound bombs. A signal lamp, adjacent to this switch, will glow when the 100-pound bombs are nose-armed.

(3) RELEASE.—Release of the bombs, as selected, is accomplished by the push-button type thumb switch *(figure 35)* located on the top of the control stick in the front cockpit. Bombs may be dropped selectively by pushing the control stick release button consecutively. The bombs are released in a definite order, from inboard to outboard and simultaneously on both sides of the airplane when both racks are used together. The "BOMB SAFETY" switch circuits and the firing switch circuits on the control stick are protected from current overloads by two 50-ampere fuses in the main switch panel. Provisions are made for a bomb control quadrant *(figure 38)* on the control shelf on the left side of the front cockpit. This quadrant provides an arming and release handle, stamped "A" and "R", respectively. The arming handle will arm the 20- and 30-pound bombs at the nose, and the 100-pound bombs at the nose or the tail. Except for nose-arming the 100-pound bombs, all arming must be done through this arming handle. The release handle when at "LOCK" position locks the entire system and will prevent release, either electrically or manually, of all bombs. The handle must be moved to "SELECTIVE" position before electrical release can be accomplished. In moving the release handle to "SALVO", all bombs are dropped simultaneously, either in the "ARMED" or "SAFE" condition, according to the setting of the arming handle and the electrical toggle switches. Provision is also made for a release handle in the rear cockpit, beneath the control shelf on the left side, which will only "SALVO" all bombs.

CAUTION

This is for use in an emergency and will release bombs either in the "SAFE" or "ARMED" condition, according to the arming handle and the electrical toggle switches in the front cockpit.

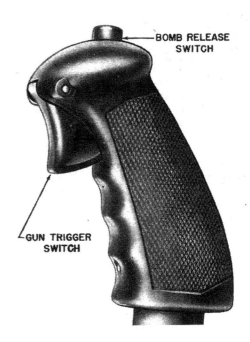

BOMB RELEASE SWITCH

GUN TRIGGER SWITCH

Figure 35 — Gun and Bomb Control Switches

b. ARMING PROCEDURE.—Nose arming is accomplished by moving the bomb arming handle to the "ARMED" position and by moving the "NOSE FUSE" switch to the "ON" position. Tail arming is accomplished by moving the arming handle to the "ARMED" position.

(1) SELECTIVE RELEASE.—To drop bombs selectively, proceed as follows:

(a) Move the bomb release handle to the "SELECTIVE" position. The knob on the release handle must be depressed to release the handle for movement.

(b) Select the rack to be used by turning "ON" the "BOMB SELECTOR" switch.

(c) Place the "BOMB SAFETY" switch in the "ON" position.

(d) Press the bomb release button on the control stick to release the bomb or bombs. Bombs may be selected for alternate release from each side of the airplane by moving the left and right "BOMB SELECTOR" switches to "ON" and "OFF" alternately.

(2) SALVO RELEASE.—If all bombs are to be dropped simultaneously, proceed as follows:

(a) Press down on the knurled salvo safety ring, located half-way down the release handle, and turn it counterclockwise. This will allow the release handle to

1. Lens Assembly   3. Adusting Knob
2. Dust Shield   4. Sight Housing

Figure 36 — Gun Sight

be moved through the "SELECTIVE" position to the "SALVO" position.

(b) All bombs will drop simultaneously, either "ARMED" or "SAFE", depending on the setting of the arming handle and the position of the nose fuse switch.

(c) Pulling the release handle in the rear cockpit will "SALVO" bombs.

3. GUNNERY EQUIPMENT.

(See figures 35, 36, 37, and 39.)

a. DESCRIPTION.—Gunnery equipment consists of complete provisions for the installation and operation of three model M-2, .30-caliber machine guns: a fuselage gun synchronized to fire through the propeller arc, a gun mounted in the right outer wing panel, and a flexible gun in the rear cockpit. Two hundred rounds of ammunition are supplied each fixed gun from a box mounted adjacent to the gun. Five 100-round ammunition boxes are installed in the rear cockpit to supply the flexible gun. A type N-3B optical gun sight is mounted in the center, directly below the front instrument panel. Gun sight light intensity

is controlled by a rheostat to decrease the intensity during night flying. Sight reticle adjustment is effected by a knurled knob on the right side of the sight assembly. Provisions are installed for a type W-7B camera to operate simultaneously with either or both fixed guns. Saftey switches for camera and gun solenoids are located on the front cockpit electrical control panel.

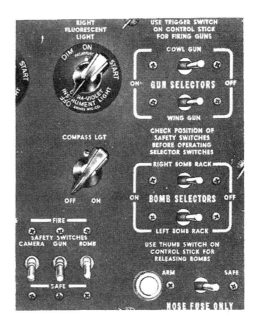

Figure 37 — Armament Control Switches

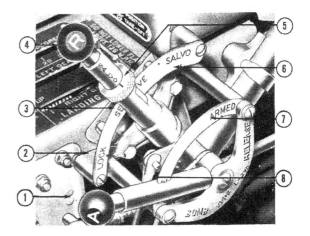

1. Arming Handle   5. Salvo Safety Ring
2. "LOCK" Position   6. "SALVO" Position
3. "SELECTIVE" Position 7. "ARMED" Position
4. Release Handle   8. "SAFE" Position

Figure 38 — Bomb Control Quadrant

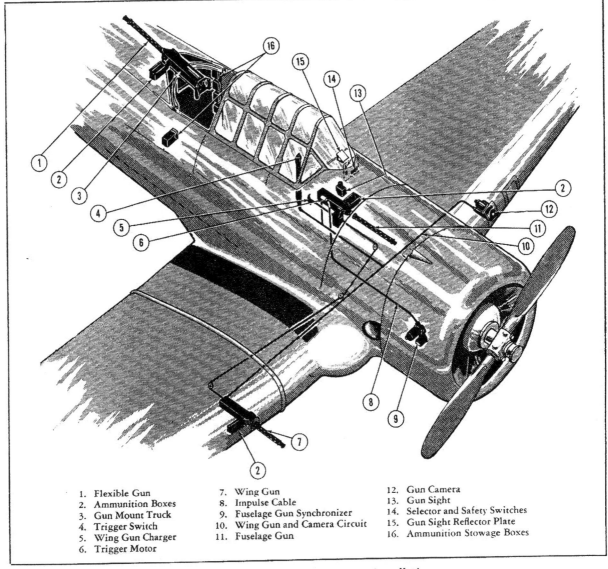

1. Flexible Gun
2. Ammunition Boxes
3. Gun Mount Truck
4. Trigger Switch
5. Wing Gun Charger
6. Trigger Motor
7. Wing Gun
8. Impulse Cable
9. Fuselage Gun Synchronizer
10. Wing Gun and Camera Circuit
11. Fuselage Gun
12. Gun Camera
13. Gun Sight
14. Selector and Safety Switches
15. Gun Sight Reflector Plate
16. Ammunition Stowage Boxes

Figure 39 — Gunnery and Camera Installation

b. OPERATION.

(1) FIXED GUNS.

(a) Charge the fuselage gun by pulling back on the charging handle on the left side of the gun.

(b) Charge the wing gun on late airplanes by pulling back on the charging handle to the right of the gun sight. Wing guns on early airplanes are manually charged when serviced.

(c) Place the selector and safety switches "FIRE."

(d) Fire the guns by squeezing the trigger on the control stick grip.

Note

Put the rear control stick in the stowed position before rotating seat.

(2) FLEXIBLE GUN.

(a) Pull outward on the gun yoke locking knob.

(b) Pull up and back on the gun until the locking knob snaps into place.

(c) Raise the truck-locking handle to move the gun truck along the track.

(d) Lower the handle at the desired position.

(e) Pull back on the charging handle and then release it.

(f) To fire the gun, press the trigger on the hand grip.

4. PHOTOGRAPHIC EQUIPMENT.

a. GUN CAMERA. *(See figure 39.)*—Complete provisions are installed for a type W-7B gun camera in the left outer-wing leading edge near the center sections. The camera is synchronized to fire with the wing or fuselage gun, or both, and is operated by the gun firing switch on the front cockpit control stick. A safety switch is located on the front cockpit electrical control panel. This switch must be in "FIRE" position before camera will operate.

b. AERIAL CAMERA.—Provisions are made for the installation and operation of a type K-3B or K-17 aerial camera and a type A-2 view finder. Controls for the camera consist of a type B-2 intervalometer, a vacuum selector valve, and two warning lights. The interval-

ometer governs the automatic operation of the camera and is provided with a control knob for setting exposures from 6 to 75 seconds apart. The vacuum selector valve is marked "ON" and "OFF". *(See figure 40.)* When "ON", vaccum holds the film to the focal plane contact glass. A signal light is located on the power junction box near the camera and on the upper front instrument panel to warn the pilot and cameraman 3 seconds before each exposure, when using the intervalometer. Camera doors are also provided below the camera mount in the rear fuselage. To open or close the camera doors, push down on the control handle located on the forward end of each door; then push or pull the handle quickly to engage the doors in an open or closed position, respectively.

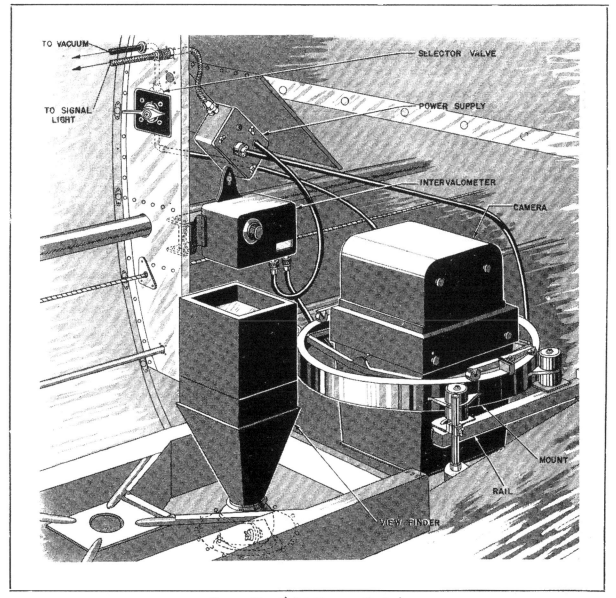

Figure 40 — Aerial Camera Controls

5. OXYGEN EQUIPMENT.

a. DESCRIPTION. *(See figure 41.)* — The high-pressure oxygen system consists of two type B-1 cylinders, two type A-8 regulators (with flow indicator and pressure gage), and the necessary tubing and fittings. The regulator units are installed on the right side of each cockpit. The front cockpit regulator is supplied oxygen by the right cylinder and the rear regulator by the left cylinder. Normal full pressure of each cylinder is 1800 lb/sq in.

b. OPERATION. — Turning the regulator control knob is the only manual operation required in high-pressure oxygen systems. Quantity of oxygen supplied is determined by the position of this control. Open the control knob until the flow indicator reading corresponds with the altitude at which the airplane is flying.

c. CONSUMPTION CHART.—The following table indicates the approximate supply of oxygen in man-hours at designated altitudes when the cylinders are fully charged.

Altitude (in Feet)	Hours Available (1 Man)
10,000	5.05
12,000	4.95
14,000	4.85
16,000	4.60
18,000	4.40
20,000	4.20
22,000	4.05
24,000	3.85
26,000	3.70

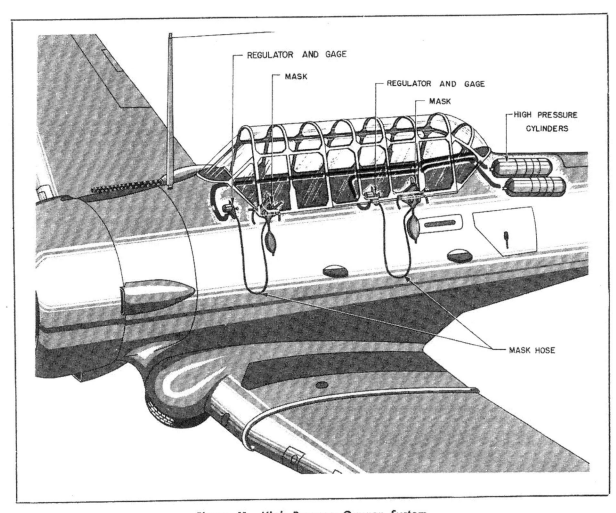

Figure 41 — High Pressure Oxygen System

APPENDIX I
FLIGHT OPERATING CHARTS

1. FLIGHT PLANNING.

a. GENERAL.

(1) A series of charts on the following pages is provided to aid in selecting the proper power and altitude to be used for obtaining optimum range of the airplane. Charts are provided for each airplane configuration with the probable ranges of gross weights.

(2) If the flight plan calls for a continuous flight where the desired cruising power and air speed are reasonably constant after take-off and climb and the external load items are the same throughout the flight, the fuel required and flight time may be computed as a single section flight. If this is not the case, the flight may be broken up into sections, and each leg of the flight planned separately, since dropping of external bombs causes considerable changes in range and air speed for given power. (Within the limits of the airplane, the fuel required and flying time for a given mission depend largely upon the speed desired. With all other factors remaining equal in an airplane, speed is obtained at a sacrifice of range, and range is obtained at a sacrifice of speed.)

b. USE OF CHARTS.

(1) Although instructions for their use are shown on the "Flight Operation Instruction Charts", the following expanded information on proper use of the charts may be helpful.

(2) Select the "Flight Operation Instruction Chart" for the model airplane, gross weight, and external loading to be used at take-off. The amount of gasoline available for flight planning purposes depends upon the reserve required and the amount required for starting and warm-up. Reserve should be based on the type of mission, terrain over which the flight is to be made, and weather conditions. The fuel required for climb and time to climb to various altitudes is shown on the "Take-Off, Climb, and Landing Chart". Fuel remaining after subtracting reserve, warm-up, and climb fuel from total amount available is the amount to be used for flight planning.

(3) Select a figure in the fuel column in the upper section of the chart equal to, or the next entry less than, the amount of fuel available for flight planning. Move horizontally to the right or left and select a figure equal to, or the next entry greater than, the distance (with no wind) to be flown. Operating values contained in the lower section of the column number in which this figure appears represent the highest cruising speeds possible at the range desired. It will be noted that the ranges listed in column I are figured for the altitude which gives the least miles per gallon. The ranges shown in column II and other columns to the right of column II can be obtained at any of the altitudes listed in the Altitude column. All of the power settings listed in a column will give approximately the same number of miles per gallon if each is used at the altitude shown on the same horizontal line with it. Note that the time required for the flight may be shortened by selection of the higher altitudes. The flight duration may be obtained by dividing the true air speed of the flight altitude into the air miles to be flown.

(4) The flight plan may be readily changed at any time en route, and the chart will show the balance of range available at various cruising powers by following the "Instructions for Using Chart" printed on each chart.

Note

The above instructions and following charts do not take into account the effect of wind. Adjustments to range values and flight duration to allow for wind may be made by any method familiar to the pilot, such as by the use of a flight calculator or a navigator's triangle of velocities.

c. SAMPLE PROBLEM.

(1) To fly 450 miles at a cruising altitude of 9000 feet with a take-off weight of 5500 pounds and no external load, the flight should be planned as follows:

(a) The fuel used for take-off and climb to 9000 feet is 15 gallons (using the data listed under 10,000 feet). Adding to this fuel the amount for landing and reserve (15 gallons) makes a total of 30 gallons not available for cruising. Thus there are 81 gallons for cruising (111—30=81).

(b) The range shown in column IV for 80 gallons is 470 miles or approximately 20 miles reserve.

(c) Vertically below in the table and opposite 10,000 feet (since 9000 feet is not listed) read 1800 rpm, full throttle, 180 mph true speed, and a fuel flow of 30 gph with the mixture in lean operation. Range to be traveled divided by true air speed equals the hours of flight (450÷180=2.5 hours). Hours multiplied by fuel flow equals the gallons used (2.5×30=75 gallons). Thus the fuel reserve is 81 less 75 or 6 gallons.

(2) As an alternate plan, reference to column V for maximum range at the extreme right of chart shows that the flight may be made with a sacrifice of 30 mph speed if more reserve is desired. The operating conditions in this case are 1600 rpm, 23 in. Hg manifold pressure, 155 mph true air speed at 23 gph fuel consumption. Under this plan, the time required will be 2.9 hours and the fuel used will be 67 gallons. Thus the time required will be .4 of an hour longer than (1) and will leave 8 gallons more for reserve.

(3) If arrival over a check point is late, because of head winds, reference to the charts and calculations will allow the pilot while in flight to select new cruising conditions for safe arrival at his destination.

TAKE-OFF, CLIMB & LANDING CHART

AIRCRAFT MODEL(S) AT-6 SNJ
ENGINE MODEL(S) R-1340-AN-1

TAKE-OFF DISTANCE — FEET

GROSS WEIGHT LB.	HEAD WIND M.P.H.	HEAD WIND KTS.	HARD SURFACE RUNWAY — AT SEA LEVEL GROUND RUN	TO CLEAR 50' OBJ.	AT 3000 FEET GROUND RUN	TO CLEAR 50' OBJ.	AT 6000 FEET GROUND RUN	TO CLEAR 50' OBJ.	SOD-TURF RUNWAY — AT SEA LEVEL GROUND RUN	TO CLEAR 50' OBJ.	AT 3000 FEET GROUND RUN	TO CLEAR 50' OBJ.	AT 6000 FEET GROUND RUN	TO CLEAR 50' OBJ.	SOFT SURFACE RUNWAY — AT SEA LEVEL GROUND RUN	TO CLEAR 50' OBJ.	AT 3000 FEET GROUND RUN	TO CLEAR 50' OBJ.	AT 6000 FEET GROUND RUN	TO CLEAR 50' OBJ.
6000	0	0	1000	1700	1300	2000	1500	2400	1100	1800	1400	2200	1600	2500	1300	2100	1700	2500	2100	3000
	17	15	700	1200	800	1400	1000	1700	700	1300	900	1500	1100	1800	900	1400	1100	1700	1400	2100
	34	30	400	800	500	900	600	1100	400	800	500	1000	700	1200	500	900	600	1100	800	1400
	51	45	200	500	200	600	300	700	200	500	300	600	400	700	300	500	300	700	500	800
5500	0	0	900	1500	1000	1800	1300	2000	900	1600	1100	1800	1400	2100	1100	1700	1400	2100	1700	2500
	17	15	500	1000	700	1200	800	1400	600	1100	700	1300	900	1500	700	1200	900	1400	1100	1700
	34	30	300	700	400	800	500	900	300	700	400	800	500	1000	400	700	500	900	700	1100
	51	45	100	400	200	500	300	600	200	400	200	500	300	600	200	400	200	500	300	700

NOTE: INCREASE CHART DISTANCES AS FOLLOWS: 75°F + 10%; 100°F + 20%; 125°F + 30%; 150°F + 40%
BASED ON: FLIGHT TESTS
DATA AS OF 8-10-44
OPTIMUM TAKE-OFF WITH 2250 RPM, 36 IN.HG. & DEG. FLAP IS 80% OF CHART VALUES

CLIMB DATA

GROSS WEIGHT LB.	AT SEA LEVEL BEST I.A.S. MPH	KTS	RATE OF CLIMB F.P.M.	GAL. OF FUEL USED	AT 5000 FEET BEST I.A.S. MPH	KTS	RATE OF CLIMB F.P.M.	FROM SEA LEVEL TIME MIN.	FUEL USED	AT 10,000 FEET BEST I.A.S. MPH	KTS	RATE OF CLIMB F.P.M.	FROM SEA LEVEL TIME MIN.	FUEL USED	AT 15,000 FEET BEST I.A.S. MPH	KTS	RATE OF CLIMB F.P.M.	FROM SEA LEVEL TIME MIN.	FUEL USED	AT 20,000 FEET BEST I.A.S. MPH	KTS	RATE OF CLIMB F.P.M.	FROM SEA LEVEL TIME MIN.	FUEL USED
6000	115	100	1050	8	115	100	1100	5.0	12	115	100	800	10.0	16	110	95	500	18.0	21	105	90	200	32	28
5500	115	100	1150	8	115	100	1200	4.5	12	115	100	900	9.0	15	110	95	550	16.0	20	105	90	250	29	26

POWER PLANT SETTINGS: (DETAILS ON FIG. 26 SECTION III):
BASED ON: FLIGHT TESTS
DATA AS OF 8-10-44

FUEL USED (U.S. GAL.) INCLUDES WARM-UP & TAKE-OFF ALLOWANCE

LANDING DISTANCE — FEET

GROSS WEIGHT LB.	BEST IAS APPROACH POWER OFF MPH	KTS	POWER ON MPH	KTS	HARD DRY SURFACE — AT SEA LEVEL GROUND ROLL	TO CLEAR 50' OBJ.	AT 3000 FEET GROUND ROLL	TO CLEAR 50' OBJ.	AT 6000 FEET GROUND ROLL	TO CLEAR 50' OBJ.	FIRM DRY SOD — AT SEA LEVEL GROUND ROLL	TO CLEAR 50' OBJ.	AT 3000 FEET GROUND ROLL	TO CLEAR 50' OBJ.	AT 6000 FEET GROUND ROLL	TO CLEAR 50' OBJ.	WET OR SLIPPERY — AT SEA LEVEL GROUND ROLL	TO CLEAR 50' OBJ.	AT 3000 FEET GROUND ROLL	TO CLEAR 50' OBJ.	AT 6000 FEET GROUND ROLL	TO CLEAR 50' OBJ.
5500	100	87	100	87	700	1600	800	1700	900	1800	800	1700	900	1800	1000	1900	1800	2700	2000	2900	2200	3100
5000	100	87	100	87	700	1500	700	1600	800	1700	700	1600	800	1700	900	1800	1600	2500	1800	2600	2000	2800

DATA AS OF 8-10-44   BASED ON: FLIGHT TESTS
OPTIMUM LANDING IS 80% OF CHART VALUES

LEGEND

I.A.S. : INDICATED AIRSPEED
M.P.H. : MILES PER HOUR
KTS. : KNOTS
F.P.M. : FEET PER MINUTE

REMARKS:
NOTE: TO DETERMINE FUEL CONSUMPTION IN BRITISH IMPERIAL GALLONS, MULTIPLY BY 10, THEN DIVIDE BY 12

AAFMC-527
11-1-44

Figure 42 — Take-off, Climb, and Landing Chart

FLIGHT OPERATION INSTRUCTION CHART

AIRCRAFT MODEL(S)
AT-6
SNJ
ENGINE(S): R-1340-AN-1

CHART WEIGHT LIMITS: 5600 TO 4500 POUNDS

EXTERNAL LOAD ITEMS
NONE

NUMBER OF ENGINES OPERATING:

INSTRUCTIONS FOR USING CHART: SELECT FIGURE IN FUEL COLUMN EQUAL TO OR LESS THAN AMOUNT OF FUEL TO BE USED FOR CRUISING. MOVE HORIZONTALLY TO RIGHT OR LEFT AND SELECT RANGE VALUE EQUAL TO OR GREATER THAN THE STATUTE OR NAUTICAL AIR MILES TO BE FLOWN. VERTICALLY BELOW AND OPPOSITE VALUE ALONE DESIRED CRUISING ALTITUDE (ALT.) READ RPM, MANIFOLD PRESSURE (M.P.) AND MIXTURE SETTING REQUIRED.

NOTES: COLUMN I IS FOR EMERGENCY HIGH SPEED CRUISING ONLY. COLUMNS II, III, IV AND V GIVE PROGRESSIVE INCREASE IN RANGE AT A SACRIFICE IN SPEED. AIR MILES PER GALLON (MI./GAL.) (NO WIND), GALLONS PER HR. (G.P.H.) AND TRUE AIRSPEED (T.A.S.) ARE APPROXIMATE VALUES FOR REFERENCE. RANGE VALUES ARE FOR AN AVERAGE AIRPLANE FLYING ALONE (NO WIND). TO OBTAIN BRITISH IMPERIAL GAL. (OR G.P.H.) MULTIPLY U.S. GAL. (OR G.P.H.) BY 10 THEN DIVIDE BY 12.

LIMITS	RPM	M.P. IN.HG.	BLOWER POSITION	MIXTURE POSITION	TIME LIMIT	CYL. TEMP.	TOTAL G.P.H.
WAR EMERG.							
MILITARY POWER	2250	36	RICH	5 MIN.	260	65

FOR DETAILS SEE POWER PLANT CHART (FIG.26 SECT.III)

SINGLE SPEED

COLUMN I

RANGE IN AIRMILES		FUEL U.S. GAL.			
STATUTE	NAUTICAL				
450	390	111 / 100			
410 380 320	350 310 270	90 80 70			
270 230 180	230 200 160	60 50 40			
130 90 40	120 80 40	30 20 10			

MAXIMUM CONTINUOUS
(4.55 STAT. (3.95 NAUT.) MI./GAL.)

R.P.M.	M.P. INCHES	MIX-TURE (2)	TOT. G.P.M.	T.A.S. MPH	KTS.	PRESS ALT. FEET
						40000 35000 30000
						25000 20000 15000
2050 1950 1950	F.T. 30 31	RICH RICH RICH	42 42 40	195 190 180	170 165 155	10000 5000 S.L.

COLUMN II

RANGE IN AIRMILES		FUEL U.S. GAL.		
STATUTE	NAUTICAL			
520	450	111 / 100		
470 410 360	400 360 310	90 80 70		
310 280 210	270 220 180	80 50 40		
160 100 50	130 90 40	30 20 10		

(5.2 STAT. (4.5 NAUT.) MI./GAL.)

R.P.M.	M.P. INCHES	MIX-TURE (2)	TOT. G.P.M.	T.A.S. MPH	KTS.	PRESS ALT. FEET
2000	F.T.	RICH	36	185	160	
2000 2000 2000	F.T. 28 30	LEAN LEAN LEAN	37 36 34	190 185 175	165 160 150	

COLUMN III

SUBTRACT FUEL ALLOWANCES NOT AVAILABLE FOR CRUISING (1)

RANGE IN AIRMILES		FUEL U.S. GAL.		
STATUTE	NAUTICAL			
590	510	111 / 100		
530 470 410	460 410 360	90 80 70		
350 290 230	300 250 200	80 50 40		
170 120 60	150 100 50	30 20 10		

(5.9 STAT. (5.15 NAUT.) MI./GAL.)

R.P.M.	M.P. INCHES	MIX-TURE (2)	TOT. G.P.M.	T.A.S. MPH	KTS.	PRESS ALT. FEET
2000	F.T.	LEAN	32	185	160	
1800 1600 1600	F.T. 29 30	LEAN LEAN LEAN	30 29 27	180 170 155	155 145 135	

COLUMN IV

COLUMN V

RANGE IN AIRMILES		FUEL U.S. GAL.		
STATUTE	NAUTICAL			
670	580	111 / 100		
600 530 470	520 460 400	90 80 70		
400 330 270	350 290 230	80 50 40		
200 130 60	170 110 60	30 20 10		

MAXIMUM AIR RANGE

R.P.M.	M.P. INCHES	MIX-TURE (2)	TOT. G.P.M.	T.A.S. MPH	KTS.	PRESS ALT. FEET
1700	F.T.	LEAN	25	165	145	
1600 1600 1600	23 24 25	LEAN LEAN LEAN	23 22 20	155 145 130	135 125 115	

SPECIAL NOTES

(1) MAKE ALLOWANCE FOR WARM-UP, TAKE-OFF & CLIMB (SEE FIG. 42.) PLUS ALLOWANCE FOR WIND, RESERVE AND COMBAT AS REQUIRED.

(2) THE MIXTURE CONTROL IN THIS AIRPLANE IS NOT AUTOMATIC AND MUST BE ADJUSTED MANUALLY TO OBTAIN SMOOTH ENGINE OPERATION AND BEST RANGE.

EXAMPLE

AT 5500 LB. GROSS WEIGHT WITH 76 GAL. OF FUEL (AFTER DEDUCTING TOTAL ALLOWANCES OF 35 GAL.) TO FLY 430 STAT. AIRMILES AT 15,000 FT. ALTITUDE MAINTAIN 2000 RPM AND F.T. IN. MANIFOLD PRESSURE WITH MIXTURE SET: LEAN.

LEGEND

ALT. : PRESSURE ALTITUDE
M.P. : MANIFOLD PRESSURE
GPM : U.S. GAL. PER HOUR
TAS : TRUE AIRSPEED
KTS. : KNOTS
S.L. : SEA LEVEL

F.R. : FULL RICH
A.R. : AUTO-RICH
A.L. : AUTO-LEAN
C.L. : CRUISING LEAN
M.L. : MANUAL LEAN
F.T. : FULL THROTTLE

RED FIGURES ARE PRELIMINARY DATA, SUBJECT TO REVISION AFTER FLIGHT CHECK

DATA AS OF: 8-10-44   BASED ON: FLIGHT TESTS

Figure 43 (Sheet 1 of 2 Sheets) — Flight Operation Instruction Chart

AAFMC-52B
8-1-44
WP-3-31-44-10M

AIRCRAFT MODEL(S) AT-6 SNJ ENGINE(S): R-1340-AN-1	FLIGHT OPERATION INSTRUCTION CHART	EXTERNAL LOAD ITEMS WING BOMBS
	CHART WEIGHT LIMITS: 6000 TO 5000 POUNDS	NUMBER OF ENGINES OPERATING: 1

LIMITS	R.P.M.	M.P. IN.HG.	BLOWER POSITION	MIXTURE POSITION	TIME LIMIT	CYL. TEMP.	TOTAL G.P.H.
WAR EMERG.			SINGLE SPEED				
MILITARY POWER	2250	36	SINGLE SPEED	RICH	5 MIN.	260	65

FOR DETAILS SEE POWER PLANT CHART (FIG. 26 SECT. III)

INSTRUCTIONS FOR USING CHART: SELECT FIGURE IN FUEL COLUMN EQUAL TO OR LESS THAN AMOUNT OF FUEL TO BE USED FOR CRUISING(1) MOVE HORIZONTALLY TO RIGHT OR LEFT AND SELECT RANGE VALUE EQUAL TO OR GREATER THAN THE STATUTE OR NAUTICAL AIR MILES TO BE FLOWN. VERTICALLY BELOW AND OPPOSITE VALUE NEAREST DESIRED CRUISING ALTITUDE (ALT.) READ RPM, MANIFOLD PRESSURE (M.P.) AND MIXTURE SETTING REQUIRED.

NOTES: COLUMN I IS FOR EMERGENCY HIGH SPEED CRUISING ONLY. COLUMNS II, III, IV AND V GIVE PROGRESSIVE INCREASE IN RANGE AT A SACRIFICE IN SPEED. AIR MILES PER GALLON (MI./GAL.) (NO WIND), GALLONS PER HR. (G.P.H.) AND TRUE AIRSPEED (T.A.S.) ARE APPROXIMATE VALUES FOR REFERENCE. RANGE VALUES ARE FOR AN AVERAGE AIRPLANE FLYING ALONE (NO WIND).(1) TO OBTAIN BRITISH IMPERIAL GAL. (OR G.P.H.): MULTIPLY U.S. GAL. (OR G.P.H.) BY 10 THEN DIVIDE BY 12.

COLUMN I Statute	COLUMN I Nautical	FUEL U.S. GAL.	COLUMN II Statute	COLUMN II Nautical	COLUMN III Statute	COLUMN III Nautical	COLUMN IV Statute	COLUMN IV Nautical	FUEL U.S. GAL.	COLUMN V Statute	COLUMN V Nautical
		111	SUBTRACT FUEL ALLOWANCES NOT AVAILABLE FOR CRUISING (1)						111		
340	300	100	430	380	500	430	550	480	100	620	540
310	270	90	390	340	450	390	500	430	90	560	480
270	240	80	350	300	400	350	440	380	80	490	430
240	210	70	300	260	350	300	390	340	70	430	370
200	180	60	260	220	300	260	330	290	60	370	320
170	150	50	220	190	250	220	270	240	50	310	270
130	120	40	170	150	200	170	220	190	40	250	210
100	90	30	130	110	150	130	160	140	30	180	160
70	60	20	80	70	100	80	110	90	20	120	100
30	30	10	40	30	50	40	50	50	10	60	50

MAXIMUM CONTINUOUS

PRESS ALT. FEET	R.P.M.	M.P. INCHES	MIXTURE (2)	APPROX. TOT. GPH.	T.A.S. MPH.	T.A.S. KTS.
40000						
35000						
30000						
25000						
20000						
15000	2200	F.T.	RICH	41	185	160
10000	2200	F.T.	RICH	48	195	170
5000	2200	F.T.	RICH	58	200	175
S.L.	2200	32.5	RICH	51	185	160

COLUMN II (4.35 STAT. (3.8 NAUT.) MI./GAL.)

PRESS ALT. FEET	R.P.M.	M.P. INCHES	MIXTURE (2)	APPROX. TOT. GPH.	T.A.S. MPH.	T.A.S. KTS.
40000						
35000						
30000						
25000						
20000						
15000						
10000	2050	F.T.	RICH	43	190	165
5000	1900	30	RICH	43	185	160
S.L.	1950	31	RICH	41	175	150

COLUMN III (5.05 STAT. (4.35 NAUT.) MI./GAL.)

PRESS ALT. FEET	R.P.M.	M.P. INCHES	MIXTURE (2)	APPROX. TOT. GPH.	T.A.S. MPH.	T.A.S. KTS.
40000						
35000						
30000						
25000						
20000						
15000	2000	F.T.	RICH	36	175	155
10000	2000	F.T.	LEAN	37	185	160
5000	2000	29	LEAN	36	180	155
S.L.	1900	30	LEAN	34	170	145

COLUMN IV (5.55 STAT. (4.8 NAUT.) MI./GAL.)

PRESS ALT. FEET	R.P.M.	M.P. INCHES	MIXTURE (2)	APPROX. TOT. GPH.	T.A.S. MPH.	T.A.S. KTS.
40000						
35000						
30000						
25000						
20000						
15000	2000	F.T.	LEAN	32	175	155
10000	1800	F.T.	LEAN	32	175	155
5000	1650	28	LEAN	30	165	145
S.L.	1600	31	LEAN	28	155	135

MAXIMUM AIR RANGE

PRESS ALT. FEET	R.P.M.	M.P. INCHES	MIXTURE (2)	APPROX. TOT. GPH.	T.A.S. MPH.	T.A.S. KTS.
40000						
35000						
30000						
25000						
20000						
15000	1750	F.T.	LEAN	25	155	135
10000	1600	24	LEAN	24	150	130
5000	1600	25	LEAN	22	135	120
S.L.	1600	26	LEAN	20	125	110

SPECIAL NOTES

(1) MAKE ALLOWANCE FOR WARM-UP, TAKE-OFF & CLIMB (SEE FIG. 42) PLUS ALLOWANCE FOR WIND, RESERVE AND COMBAT AS REQUIRED.

(2) THE MIXTURE CONTROL IN THIS AIRPLANE IS NOT AUTOMATIC AND MUST BE ADJUSTED MANUALLY TO OBTAIN SMOOTH ENGINE OPERATION AND BEST RANGE.

EXAMPLE

AT 6000 LB. GROSS WEIGHT WITH 75 GAL. OF FUEL (AFTER DEDUCTING TOTAL ALLOWANCES OF 36 GAL.) TO FLY 450 STAT. AIRMILES AT 15,000 FT. ALTITUDE MAINTAIN 1750 RPM AND F.T. IN. MANIFOLD PRESSURE WITH MIXTURE SET: LEAN.

LEGEND

ALT. : PRESSURE ALTITUDE
M.P. : MANIFOLD PRESSURE
GPH : U.S.GAL. PER HOUR
TAS : TRUE AIRSPEED
KTS. : KNOTS
S.L. : SEA LEVEL
F.R. : FULL RICH
A.R. : AUTO-RICH
A.L. : AUTO-LEAN
C.L. : CRUISING LEAN
M.L. : MANUAL LEAN
F.T. : FULL THROTTLE

DATA AS OF *8-10-44* BASED ON: *FLIGHT TEST*

RED FIGURES ARE PRELIMINARY DATA, SUBJECT TO REVISION AFTER FLIGHT CHECK

Figure 43 (Sheet 2 of 2 Sheets)—Flight Operation Instruction Chart

WARSHIPS DVD SERIES

WARSHIPS: CARRIER MISHAPS

AIRCRAFT CARRIER
MISHAPS
SAFETY AND TRAINING FILMS

-PERISCOPEFILM.COM-

DVD

NOW AVAILABLE ON DVD!

AIRCRAFT AT WAR
DVD SERIES

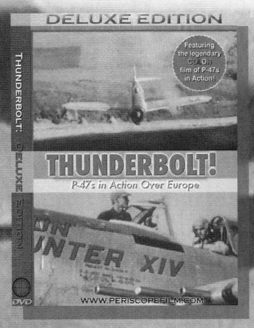

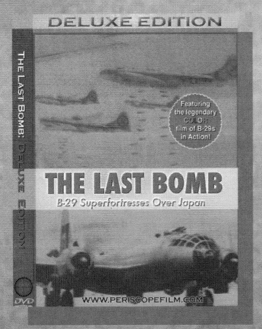

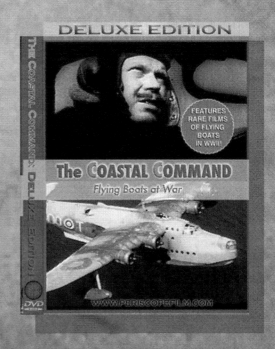

NOW AVAILABLE!

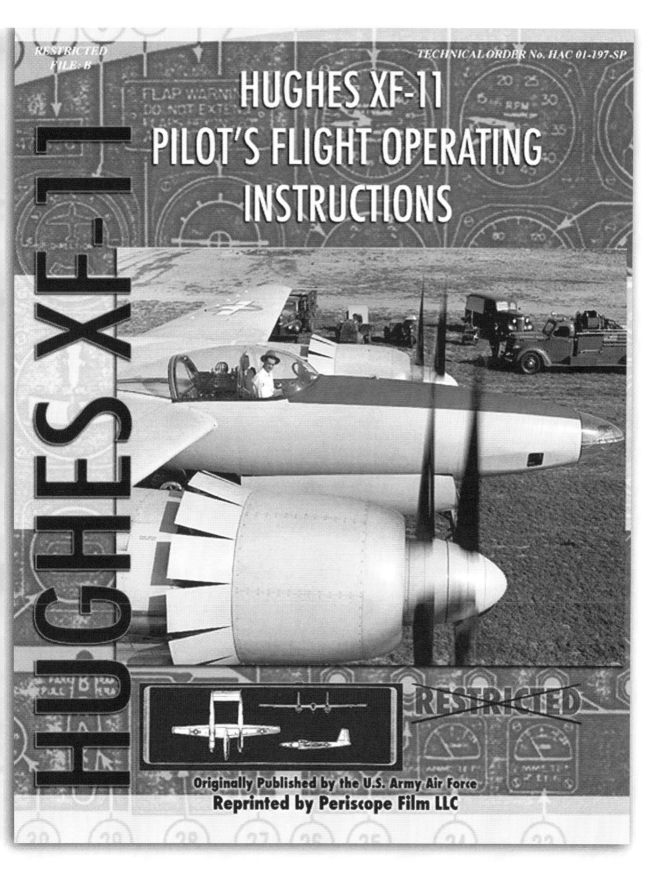

RESTRICTED
FILE: B

TECHNICAL ORDER No. HAC 01-197-SP

HUGHES XF-11 PILOT'S FLIGHT OPERATING INSTRUCTIONS

FLAP WARNIN
DO NOT EXTEN

HUGHES XF-11

RESTRICTED

Originally Published by the U.S. Army Air Force
Reprinted by Periscope Film LLC

NOW AVAILABLE!

SPRUCE GOOSE

HUGHES FLYING BOAT MANUAL

~~RESTRICTED~~

Originally Published by the War Department
Reprinted by Periscope Film LLC

NOW AVAILABLE!

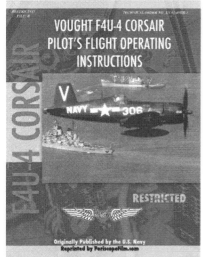
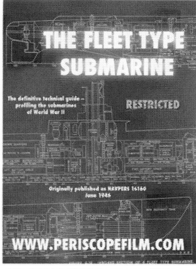

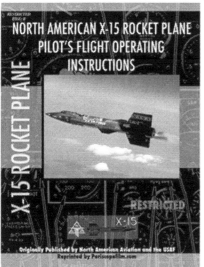
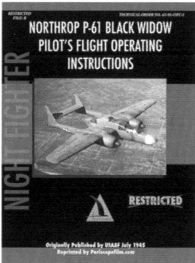
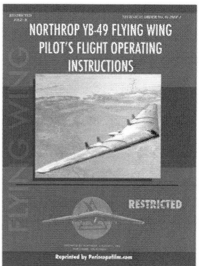
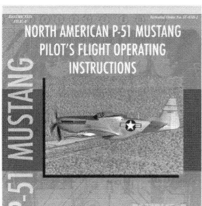

Printed in Great Britain
by Amazon

43361288R00036